Hear Her Voice

Hear Her Voice

Preaching the Women of the Bible

Christine Redwood

FOREWORD BY
Michael Frost

CASCADE *Books* · Eugene, Oregon

HEAR HER VOICE
Preaching the Women of the Bible

Cascade Books
An Imprint of Wipf and Stock Publishers
199 W. 8th Ave., Suite 3
Eugene, OR 97401

www.wipfandstock.com

PAPERBACK ISBN: 978-1-6667-8094-9
HARDCOVER ISBN: 978-1-6667-8095-6
EBOOK ISBN: 978-1-6667-8096-3

Cataloguing-in-Publication data:

Names: Redwood, Christine, author. | Frost, Michael, foreword.

Title: Hear her voice : preaching the women of the Bible / by Christine Redwood ; foreword by Michael Frost.

Description: Eugene, OR: Cascade Books, 2024 | Includes bibliographical references.

Identifiers: ISBN 978-1-6667-8094-9 (paperback) | ISBN 978-1-6667-8095-6 (hardcover) | ISBN 978-1-6667-8096-3 (ebook)

Subjects: LCSH: Preaching. | Bible. Judges—Criticism, interpretation, etc. | Feminism—Religious aspects.

Classification: BS521.4 R40 2024 (paperback) | BS521.4 (ebook)

VERSION NUMBER 07/26/24

I dedicate this work to my family, particularly my nieces, who remind me that there is a life beyond work and study. To Dave—you have come into my life unexpectedly and enriched it; thank you for your support and love. And to my sisters in Christ. Your stories continue to inspire me. May you know that you are loved and called by God and continue to lift up your voices. You have so much to contribute. I am privileged to serve alongside so many of you.

Contents

Foreword

I'VE BEEN LISTENING TO sermons for many decades now. I don't, however, recall very many of them. Which is okay. I don't remember what I ate for dinner last Wednesday, but it nourished me and kept me warm and satisfied. Sermons are like that. The details might be forgotten but they feed the congregations who hear them and draw them nearer to God.

But there are certain sermons, like certain gourmet meals, that I can't forget. I'm sure you can think of talks or homilies that you can still remember years later—sermons that stimulated your imagination, thrilled your soul, and evoked such a response they stay with you. There haven't been too many of those for me, but Christine Redwood has delivered more than one of them. You see, Dr. Redwood is my pastor. Her sermon series on the book of Judges was indeed memorable, and her particular message on the story of Jephthah's daughter still rings in my imagination. Our whole congregation was floored by that one.

So, you can imagine my delight when I heard she was writing a book about her homiletical method. Originally coming from a conservative evangelical perspective, Christine Redwood's exploration of feminist scholarship and its application to a text like Judges lies at the heart of her work in this volume. What she distills is useful for all preachers. She points out the ways that many preachers mistakenly speak about what it means to be human through what it means to be male, and the ways female preachers can inadvertently adopt such an androcentric perspective. And, let's face it, a text like Judges gives them plenty of fodder to do so.

What Dr. Redwood's research has led her to is a counter-coherence approach that motivates her to want to help us hear the minor voices in the Scriptures. She urges us to consider choosing to identify with a minor (usually female) character in the biblical narrative and amplify that voice, which, she believes, will shape an environment wherein the minor voices in the church and wider community are similarly highlighted.

And this is key to her homiletic. Highlighting minor characters isn't done merely to entertain a congregation with often overlooked stories. In Dr. Redwood's approach it is done in order to put exegesis and application into dialogue. The preacher stands in the middle of a conversation between the biblical text and their congregation. In that intersection between a preacher, the biblical text, and the listeners, application involves reorienting the congregation to the "other" in a stance of radical compassion. The voiceless or overlooked characters bring certain realities into stark relief in ways that the better known no longer do.

In this way, Christine Redwood's congregation, of which I am part, hear the stories not only of Othniel, Samson, Barak, and Gideon, but also those of Achsah, Jael, Sisera, Delilah, and Jephthah's nameless daughter. Concerning this latter character, if she appears in sermons at all it is usually to commend her for her compliance to her father's disastrously foolish vow. She is the "good girl" who goes along with his folly. But in a sermon by Christine Redwood, she becomes a cautionary tale. Jephthah's daughter's story is told so that such an atrocious story will not be possible in the future. It is told to call out male hubris, to expose cruel intentions and selfish ambition. And in calling it out, Dr. Redwood is announcing there are times when she (and other female preachers) can't be good girls. They must resist a world in which young women are crushed within the gears of male ego and pride.

Like I said earlier, that sermon had an enormous impact in our congregation.

Many of us in the evangelical world have become used to simplistic sermons that offer us, say, "the three life lessons from the story of Gideon." These sermons put forward life principles for privileged people with autonomy and agency. We're less used to exploring the deft and intricate maneuvers required of a woman like Achsah in ancient Israel's patrilineal system. Like Delilah (or Ruth, Tamar, and the daughters of Zelophehad), Achsah succeeds in gaining some security for her family despite her vulnerability within the patriarchal system, and hearing her voice alerts us to the endlessly risky negotiation required of the weak and helpless.

I commend this book to you as an important contribution to the study of homiletics. Christine Redwood's sermons are demanding, stimulating, playful, and practical. And here she presents her scholarship as winsomely in print as she does in the pulpit. At a time when a woman's role in the pulpit is still keenly contested, particularly in evangelical circles, Christine Redwood is an emerging voice worth hearing. She draws unashamedly from her evangelical roots but is unafraid to enter into conversation with feminist hermeneutics and postcolonial theology which has helped her to develop her unique "kaleidoscopic approach."

I think this book will encourage female and male preachers from different traditions around the world while providing important insights for all pastors committed to preaching the biblical text well.

Michael Frost, Morling College, Sydney

Acknowledgments

THANK YOU TO CASCADE Books and Rodney Clapp for agreeing to take on a newcomer and publish this work. This book draws from my thesis, which I spent six years researching and preaching. I would like to thank and acknowledge those who have supported me. Andrew Sloane, not only are you brilliant, but you pastorally cared and prayed for me and stopped me from quitting! You have contributed to my formation as an academic, pastor, and a person. I am so blessed that you agreed to be my principal supervisor. Melinda Cousins, I am glad we met at the Evangelical Women in Academia Conference. You are a role model and have helped clarify my thinking and taught me much about commas! Grenville Kent, I love your creativity and giving such encouraging feedback. I am thankful for Morling College and their support—particularly for giving me opportunities to teach and also providing me with a scholarship to finish my last year as a PhD student. I am also grateful for my church community, Seaforth Baptist, and their willingness to listen to a twelve-week preaching series on the book of Judges. And lastly, thank you to Mike Frost—for taking a chance of me as a preaching intern all those years ago and continuing to champion female pastors.

1

How do we read the Bible and why does it matter?

WHEN I WAS NINETEEN years old, I attended an evangelical church near a university in Canberra. I remember sitting in a lecture hall and hearing a male preacher teach that women could not preach to a "mixed congregation" (meaning to both men and women). He declared, "That's what the Bible says." At that point, I had only ever heard one woman preach when I was a child, so I assumed he was right even though I was uncomfortable. The next time I heard a woman preach, a few years after that sermon in Canberra, I was shocked. I examined her words carefully, searching for heresy. Then, I started studying at a theological college. I began to hear women's and men's voices saying they loved the Bible and believed that women could preach. My senior pastor encouraged me to give a sermon. I began to learn how to use my voice to communicate the gospel. I also found myself in the middle of a debate still raging in evangelical churches and colleges in Australia about whether women's voices like mine should be heard from the pulpit. This time, it was more personal. But I do not want to focus on this rather old and tired question, apart from highlighting that how we read the Bible deeply matters because it can impact lives like mine.

After preaching for several years, I realized my preaching role models and theology had predominantly come from men. They were the ones reading the Bible and teaching me how to interpret and communicate it. Yet the voices that shaped me sounded in a different octave to mine. I wanted to grow beyond my initial limitations, so I embarked on further academic study, working on a PhD thesis from which this book draws. Evangelical preachers are both theologians and practitioners. I believe our experience can contribute to academic hermeneutical discussions, and the academy can contribute to growing preachers in our craft. Yet, as many have noted, there is a gap between the church and the academy.[1] Rigorous interdisciplinary work is desperately needed, particularly for preachers. Whenever someone preaches, whether they realize it or not, they stand in an intersection, drawing on various disciplines. How a preacher reads the Bible will shape the way they preach it. This is a complex space. Yet rather than engaging in this complexity, the academy tends to offer little to preachers, and preachers have little opportunity to provide their knowledge and experience to the academy.[2] Academics can sneer at preachers for abandoning theology in favor of more practical "pastoral techniques," yet as McGrath discovers, preachers can leave academic theology behind because it fails "to make the connections" that matter most to local congregations.[3] The preacher and the academic theologian can end up down very different roads. It can feel like "two diverging worlds," lament Hiestand and Wilson.[4] Preachers are meant to be theologians ensuring the "theological integrity of the people of God," yet this role tends to be given to scholars who take the title *theologian*.[5] I have experienced this disconnect as I have tried to work in both the local church while studying and occasionally teaching at an academic theological institution. There is an ongoing struggle for preachers to find ways to use academic biblical scholarship and connect it to church practices like sermons.[6]

1. Dunn suggests this is because evangelical Christians can be suspicious of academic scholarship. See Dunn, "Bible and Scholarship." Hiestand and Wilson provide some historical context in explaining how the gap developed; see Hiestand and Wilson, *Pastor Theologian*. Noll also writes about how "evangelicalism" had "little intellectual muscle." See Noll, *Scandal of the Evangelical Mind*, 3.

2. Wright, *Telling God's Story*, 16–17.

3. McGrath, "Futures of Evangelicalism," 16–17.

4. Hiestand and Wilson, *Pastor Theologian*, 11. Alston and Jarvis also address the need to develop pastor-theologians. See Alston and Jarvis, *Power to Comprehend*.

5. Hiestand and Wilson, *Pastor Theologian*, 19.

6. These two pieces are fifty years apart and nothing has changed—the problems persist. See Ebeling, *Theology and Proclamation*, 14; Gignilliat and Pennington, "Theological Commentary," 237.

I have dedicated six years to listening and interacting with feminist biblical scholars. Non-evangelical feminist hermeneutics tend to exist primarily in the academy and thus remain separated from the evangelical church.[7] A small qualitative study undertaken in 2013 in the US sought to examine the influence of feminist thought on the local church by having people read Judges 11 before answering a series of questions. The researcher, Milne, concludes there is "no evidence of direct awareness of any feminist studies of this text in the responses of any of the readers."[8] Yet, I believe feminist scholars have much to contribute to evangelical preaching. First, interpreters from a non-evangelical feminist perspective can raise people's awareness of how gender informs our interpretation. This question has often been posed to me as a female preacher, but it is one I have felt ill-equipped to answer. Feminist hermeneutics can provide a helpful framework.[9] Second, preachers seeking to connect with a wide range of listeners cannot anticipate all the various responses people will have to the Bible. Feminism as a broad movement has impacted contemporary Australian culture.[10] I agree with Hall that part of a theologian's (and preacher's) task is understanding their culture.[11] Engaging with feminist scholars can help preachers understand their listeners more.[12] These scholars encouraged me as I hope to encourage other female evangelical preachers to continue developing their voices and speaking, for they need to be heard. It is not an easy intersection to occupy, yet homiletics can be enriched by adding feminist voices into the mix.[13] But before we learn from them, we need to think about how we read and interpret the Bible. This is an essential task for all preachers.

7. Milne, "Margins to the Margins," 212.

8. Milne, "Margins to the Margins," 231.

9. Bond points out it can also raise tensions and make a female preacher uncomfortable or at odds with her congregation. See Bond, *Trouble with Jesus*, 9.

10. Recent news articles show the debate between feminists and hierarchical evangelicals. See Tyler, "Dangerous Doctrine." Also, Aune, "Why Feminists Are Less Religious."

11. Hall, "World's Story," 48.

12. Long, *Witness of Preaching*, 87.

13. This tension is explored further here: Hoggard Creegan and Pohl, *Living on the Boundaries*.

What We Bring to the Bible

When it comes to preaching the biblical text, I approach the text with certain presuppositions. For instance, I come to the Bible as an evangelical Christian.[14] This can be both an obvious and confusing label since even the word "evangelical" represents quite a broad camp. Many of the presuppositions I will outline do not belong exclusively to evangelicals but are shared across various Christian traditions.[15] Stackhouse provides a helpful summary by stating that evangelicals are Christocentric, biblicist, conversionist, missional, and transdenominational Christians.[16] The crucial point for preachers in Stackhouse's definition is the central role of the Bible.[17] For evangelicals, the Bible is not an ordinary book. It is the inspired Word of God.[18] I take the position that there is a God who desires to communicate good news with human beings and has done so through the Bible.[19] For evangelicals, the theological task is to be attentive to these Scriptures with a "desire to express and communicate what is to be found there to the church and to the world."[20]

Many scholars have contemplated what it means for the Bible to be called the Word of God. Wolterstorff argues that we should first approach the Bible to understand the human discourse and then the divine discourse.[21] The Bible is considered the Word of God because Yahweh has

14. At least I did when I initially started thinking about my faith tradition. Engaging with others beyond this faith tradition I'm now less sure I am welcome in the evangelical tribe or indeed if I want to be identified with this label. I will use it throughout this book although I revisit my changing stance at the end.

15. Australian evangelicalism is different from US evangelicalism, which has become a politicized term. Australian evangelicalism has tended to be shaped by both the US and British forms of evangelicalism. To read more about the history of Australian evangelicalism, see Dickey, "Evangelical Anglicans Compared."

16. Stackhouse, "Generic Evangelicalism," 124. For a broader discussion detailing the range of views concerning evangelicalism, see Naselli and Hansen, eds., Four Views. Bebbington along similar lines to Stackhouse has famously argued that evangelicals share four characteristics: conversionism (people need to change), activism (active in promoting the gospel), biblicism (a strong regard for the Bible), and crucicentrism (focus on the cross). See Bebbington, "Nature of Evangelical Religion," 33–34. Noll traces the history of the rise of this movement in his book Rise of Evangelicalism.

17. Stackhouse, "Generic Evangelicalism," 119.

18. Hodges, "New Dimensions," 210.

19. Vanhoozer, Meaning, 161.

20. McGrath, "Futures of Evangelicalism," 20.

21. Wolterstorff, Divine Discourse.

authorized it by enabling and deputizing human authors to communicate, and it is through this whole discourse known as the Bible that God speaks.[22] God, who transcends our human words, nevertheless chooses to endorse these particular words to communicate. Evangelicals trust that God's Spirit has been present through the whole process, from those who wrote it down to those who edited it to the communities who gathered these texts together, forming the biblical canon.[23] These Scriptures are not just for the original readers but for subsequent generations.[24] Evangelical preachers regard the Bible as still relevant for people today, which is why they preach from it. Osborne argues that for Christians "the final goal of hermeneutics . . . is the sermon."[25] This might be overstating the importance of the sermon, but it is true that an evangelical preacher wants to work out the significance of the biblical text for today and then proclaim it to others. The Bible is considered an authoritative text for evangelicals, which they seek to submit to and live by.[26]

Evangelicals, therefore, affirm that the Bible is truthful and trustworthy. Yet the nature of what it means for the Bible to be reliable and true has generated considerable debate. Evangelicals differ on what it means for the Bible to be true. Many defend the position known as inerrancy, although what people mean when they use the word "inerrancy" is also quite varied.[27] It could mean that the Bible is "without error" including in matters relating to scientific and historical content as well as faith and practice.[28] Or it could mean it is true on the subject it addresses, namely "things necessary to salvation" rather than science.[29] This discussion has impacted evangelical preaching, with inerrancy becoming particularly connected to expository preaching. MacArthur states an evangelical preacher should preach "in such a way that the meaning of the Bible passage is presented

22. Wolterstorff, *Divine Discourse*, 47–53.

23. Goldingay, *Interpretation of Scripture*, 104. It should be noted that there are several biblical canons. Evangelicals follow the Protestant tradition and affirm sixty-six books as canon.

24. Wolterstorff, *Divine Discourse*, 56, 131; Millar and Campbell, *Saving Eutychus*, 80.

25. Osborne, *Hermeneutical Spiral*, 29.

26. Thompson, *Preaching Biblically*, 42–43.

27. Key texts for those wanting to explore the inerrancy debate further are Warfield and Craig, *Inspiration and Authority*; Lindsell, *Battle for the Bible*; "Chicago Statement"; Merrick et al., eds., *Five Views*; Dockery and Wise, "Biblical Inerrancy."

28. Helm, "Idea of Inerrancy," 899; Lindsell, *Battle for the Bible*.

29. Packer, "*Fundamentalism*," 96–97.

entirely and exactly as it was intended by God."[30] Along similar lines, Hodges concludes that a preacher subscribing to inerrancy puts the Bible first, ahead of "personal style or charisma."[31] This gives a preacher the confidence to proclaim the "objective declarations of an omniscient God."[32] Such a sentiment, as should become clear, is not that simple. This spiraling debate has reached a tiresome impasse.[33] Thiselton proposes a more helpful approach, moving away from the language of inerrancy. Instead, he describes the Bible as an "authentic communicative act."[34] This act is both valid and "temporally conditional" because the author, text, and reader are located in time.[35] All interpretations await God's verdict at the end of history.[36] While acknowledging many stances a person can adopt when reading the Bible, evangelicals (and, more broadly, Christians) seek to take a stance of trust.[37] This does not mean hard questions cannot be asked about the text or interpretations of the text, but questions are asked with the desire to know what the text means.

As an evangelical preacher, I also approach the Bible with a focus on Jesus. While I seek to listen to the author through the text to grasp the divine intentions that have been communicated,[38] this is not done in isolation, but rather individual biblical texts are understood in relation to the whole Bible, creating a "circular relationship."[39] How a particular text fits within the wider canon is crucial for evangelical preachers. For instance, when approaching the Old Testament, I operate "within the framework of the evangel," the good news concerning Jesus Christ.[40] To borrow Enns's somewhat controversial term, I read "christotelically."[41] In other words, as an evangelical, I always read the Old Testament narrative with one eye

---

30. MacArthur, "Mandate of Biblical Inerrancy," 4.

31. Hodges, "New Dimensions," 233.

32. Hodges, "New Dimensions," 233.

33. Thiselton, "Authority and Hermeneutics," 108. Noll concurs, saying that such arguments tend to overshadow the many ways evangelicals actually agree and uphold the doctrine of inspiration. See Noll, *Between Faith and Criticism*, 145.

34. Thiselton, "Authority and Hermeneutics," 123.

35. Thiselton, "Authority and Hermeneutics," 123, 137.

36. Thiselton, "Authority and Hermeneutics," 137.

37. Briggs, *Virtuous Reader*, 103–33.

38. Brown, *Scripture as Communication*, 254.

39. Gadamer, *Truth and Method*, 182.

40. Goldingay, *Key Questions*, 238.

41. Enns, *Inspiration and Incarnation*, 154.

toward the climax, Jesus Christ.[42] Enns argues that this is how the New Testament writers interpreted the Old Testament. While we might not employ the exact hermeneutical methods the apostles engaged, evangelicals read the Old Testament as culminating in Jesus' death and resurrection; this is part of our hermeneutic.[43] Along similar lines, Kuruvilla describes the ideal preaching as being "christiconic," meaning that it should seek to facilitate the "confirmation of the children of God into the image of the Son of God."[44] In other words, preaching is meant to help believers mature in their faith and display Christlike character. Jesus Christ is essential to evangelical preaching and interpretation.

Evangelical preachers also emphasize the role of the Holy Spirit in helping people to know Christ.[45] The claim is that God speaks through the Bible by the work of the Spirit.[46] This is not a new belief nor one restricted to evangelicals; many key Christian thinkers have talked about the role of the Spirit.[47] As evangelicals take up certain habits like trust and humility, they do so to create a space for the Spirit to be at work. One way humility can be expressed is through a willingness to listen to various people and their interpretations while at the same time being "opened to being reshaped by the Spirit through the Scripture."[48] This means there is a willingness to let go of even our most treasured traditions or experiences.[49] This is the ideal; humility is not always practiced or valued by all evangelical preachers. A humble preacher recognizes that the Spirit "indigenizes the Bible's message" into a variety of cultures and transforms those cultures by allowing Scripture to critique them.[50] This is the work of application: the Spirit convicts people to trust and follow Jesus.[51]

---

42. Enns, *Inspiration and Incarnation*, 154. See also Bartholomew, "Philosophy," 62; Boda, "Biblical Theology," 144; Boyd, *Crucifixion*, 43.

43. Enns, *Inspiration and Incarnation*, 158.

44. Kuruvilla, *Manual for Preaching*, 30.

45. Goldsworthy, *Preaching the Whole Bible*, 85; Crotts, *Illuminated Preaching*.

46. Achtemeier, "Voice of the Living God"; Thompson, *Preaching Biblically*, 43.

47. There are many key theologians who have written on this: Calvin, *Institutes*, 26–30; Brown, *Holy Spirit*; DelCogliano et al., eds.,*Works on the Spirit*, 124.

48. Billings, *Word of God*, 141.

49. Though Campbell critiques evangelical theology for placing its theological framework over and above the Bible, see Campbell, *Jesus V. Evangelicals*, 78.

50. Billings, *Word of God*, 122–23.

51. John 14:26; Eph 1:17; 1 Thess 1:5.

While evangelicals hold much in common, there are passionate disputes about understanding and applying biblical texts to many contemporary issues, including gender. I am an evangelical egalitarian.[52] In response to cultural shifts in Western society, including the rise of feminism, evangelicals had to reread the Bible.[53] Feminism began as a political and intellectual movement seeking to gain equal rights for women in society through the law and by economic means. Long-established presuppositions regarding gender were challenged in all areas, including religion. There was a growing realization and critique that the roles of women and men in the public and private spheres were riddled with sexism. Sexism can be defined as a view that shapes how people perceive one another and which "benefit one sex and harm the other."[54] Feminists use the term "patriarchy" to define societies that institutionalize structures that endorse "male domination and female subordination."[55] Evangelicals responded to the rise of feminism in several ways.

As they reread the Bible, some evangelicals discovered support for women's equality in the Scriptures.[56] Genesis 1–3 is crucial in this reading. Egalitarians understand these stories as establishing that women and men are created ontologically and functionally equal; the ideal is "a relationship of mutuality."[57] For egalitarians, the patriarchal culture that predominates in the rest of the Bible (and contemporary society) is a consequence of sin, from which Jesus ultimately sets people free. The Bible, therefore, has a story of redemption for women and men.[58] In light of the work of Jesus, egalitarians affirm that women can hold leadership positions in all spheres of life, including the church.[59]

Other evangelicals read the Bible, particularly Genesis 1–3, and come to very different conclusions.[60] These evangelicals, frequently termed (hi-

52. Key evangelical egalitarian texts include Bilezikian, *Beyond Sex Roles*; Pierce and Groothuis, eds., *Discovering Biblical Equality*; Grenz and Kjesbo, *Women in the Church*.

53. Tuohy, "History of Feminist Theology," 222.

54. O'Connor, "Feminist Movement," 7.

55. Trible, "Five Loaves and Two Fishes," 280.

56. Kostenberger, *Jesus and the Feminists*, 132.

57. Bilezikian, *Beyond Sex Roles*, 17–28.

58. Parry, "Feminist Hermeneutics," 49. See also Bessey, *Jesus Feminist*; Giles, *What the Bible Actually Teaches*.

59. For a more detailed argument see Grenz and Kjesbo, *Women in the Church*.

60. Key complementarian texts include Grudem and Piper, *Recovering Biblical Manhood*; Smith, *God's Good Design*.

erarchical) complementarians, would argue that Genesis 1–3 should be understood as saying that women and men are created equal but differentiated by a functional hierarchical order.[61] In the church, the pattern established in Genesis 1–3 is now the pattern forever: "male leadership and female submission."[62] Moore goes even further and argues that "Christianity is undergirded by a vision of patriarchy"; he calls complementarians to embrace the word "patriarchy" as a good thing.[63] For complementarians, feminism is viewed as a harmful movement, a consequence of sin that "has not brought women satisfaction."[64]

While a case can clearly be made for both perspectives, I am convinced that the egalitarian position better makes sense of the whole biblical narrative. Complementarians seem to approach the Bible and view it as a static text with timeless principles that we then impose onto our context. They ignore the way they have been shaped by our cultural context and how that informs their interpretations.[65] Most complementarians do not stop women from working in senior leadership positions in the workplace, and complementarians draw different lines between what women can and cannot do, exposing how subjective and absurd these rules can be. Whereas for me, the Bible is a more dynamic text. We hear different voices and see women in a range of positions. There is a startling affirmation of women from Jesus as he enables and calls them to serve in a whole range of roles. This is good news that women still need to hear in our context as we continue to wrestle with what it looks like to follow Jesus.

What We Bring to the Bible Matters

Every preacher has presuppositions. This doesn't just apply to evangelical Christians. No preacher is neutral.[66] In the past, preachers reported being

61. Grudem, *Evangelical Feminism*, 102–30.

62. Smith, *God's Good Design*, 36–37; Strachan, "Divine Order."

63. Moore, "After Patriarchy, What?," 572.

64. Kassian, *Feminist Mistake*, 299.

65. Benckhuysen recovers the way female interpreters have understood Eve and challenged traditional male interpretations. See Benckhuysen, *Gospel According to Eve*. Barr traces the history of complementarianism arguing it too has developed from a particular historical moment. See Barr, *Making of Biblical Womanhood*.

66. Evangelical preachers sometimes neglect this. R. C. Sproul, for example, in his defense of inerrancy seems to stress that by using the grammatico-historical method the correct reading will appear. See Sproul, *Scripture Alone*, 170.

taught to appear neutral by never using the first-person pronoun in their sermons.[67] Similarly, academic work once shied away from the use of the first-person pronoun to appear objective.[68] Objectivity has, at times, been highly valued and sought after. The Reformers, for instance, valued objectivity but defined it as the effort to make the Bible their object, the object to which they submit all their thoughts, presuppositions, and traditions to be tested.[69] However, they do not always admit how hard this is to do. When our presuppositions are unexamined or unacknowledged, our interpretations can appear as a "neutral, objective analysis."[70] While I aim to be both critical and self-critical, I have deliberately chosen to use the first-person pronoun in this book to remind you I am not claiming to write an "objective" piece about the Bible and preaching.[71] Sakenfeld writes that using the first-person pronoun is critical when it comes to "any mutual engagement across dividing lines."[72] We need to recognize and name what we bring to the Bible before we can interact with others.

Gadamer affirms we are not isolated individuals interpreting a text without any prior views interfering with our understanding. All preachers approach the text with preunderstandings or "fore-projections"; we come with "particular expectations regarding certain meaning."[73] This interaction with non-Christian philosophical sources, like Gadamer, is another sign of certain presuppositions I hold. I am implicitly affirming that there is value in listening to a range of theological and philosophical voices. This is a position not shared by all evangelical Christians.[74] Indeed, some

67. Buchanan, "'I' in Sermons."

68. By objective, I mean here the attempt or the belief that someone can be an unbiased and neutral outsider who simply can get to the truth. This is what foundationalist philosophies claim to do. See Sloane, *On Being a Christian*, 16–17.

69. Torrance, *Theological Science*, 75.

70. Bartholomew, "Philosophy," 49.

71. The word "objective" does have several different meanings. I use this word here to mean I am not writing an impartial, neutral, and bias-free book. I am not claiming a God's eye view.

72. Sakenfeld, "Whose Text Is It?," 6.

73. Gadamer, *Truth and Method*, 279.

74. As noted by Stackhouse, *Need to Know*, 106; Gushee, *After Evangelicalism*, 47. Van Til is an example of someone who is critical of non-Christian epistemologies, arguing they have nothing in common with Christian epistemology and in fact, they ultimately lead to destruction. Interestingly, Van Til also affirms that nobody is neutral. He emphasizes that Christian presuppositions are the only correct and consistently reasonable view. Van Til, *Defense of the Faith*, 100–102, 201.

evangelicals would reject the notion that tradition and reason should play a major role in interpretation. It is the Bible alone that should shape our understanding.[75] This is a rather naive view and dangerous. Unacknowledged presuppositions are likely to distort interpretation and shut down the possibility of dialogue.[76]

McCaulley gives an example of the bias we can bring to the text. He writes as a Black man who studied at a predominately White evangelical college. There, he experienced "a certain disdain for what they see as the 'uncouthness' of Black culture."[77] Some White evangelicals ignored or downplayed issues around racism. McCaulley reveals one area where evangelicals can be blind. He works through this tension by articulating what Black ecclesial interpretation can bring to both the Black and White evangelical church. He begins by arguing that social location matters—African Americans' social location started in slavery, which "caused them to read the Bible differently" than slave owners.[78] Our social location is important. For example, I am not just an evangelical preacher. I could go further and say I am an Australian working in the Baptist tradition, university educated, Generation Y, Eurasian, female, living in the twenty-first century.

The preacher is "an essential and ineradicable part of the hermeneutical equation."[79] This need not be seen as a negative. Hirsch seems to think that Gadamer's use of the word "prejudice" implies the "idea of a preferred or habitual stance" that "cannot alter."[80] But Gadamer's definition of prejudice is having some opinion or judgment on an issue before considering the whole situation.[81] This can be based on prior knowledge that you might have about a text. We can have helpful and not so helpful presuppositions.[82] Homileticians intuitively understand the role of the preacher. They will often stress how the person who preaches does so through their

---

75. Goldsworthy, *Preaching the Whole Bible*, 11. Also, Van Til, *Defense of the Faith*, 226.

76. Thiselton, *Two Horizons*, 315.

77. McCaulley, *Reading While Black*, 11.

78. McCaulley, *Reading While Black*, 17.

79. Porter, "Authority of the Bible," 317.

80. Hirsch, *Validity in Interpretation*, 260.

81. Gadamer, *Truth and Method*, 283. For the German version of the text, see *Wahrheit Und Methode*, 55. The translated word "prejudice" is the German word "vorurteil" and literally means "pre-judge." S.v. "Vorurteil," in *German-English, English-German*, 669. 4th ed. Glasgow: HarperCollins, 2003.

82. Gadamer, *Truth and Method*, 289.

experiences and personality, situated in a community of believers, which, along with the work of the Spirit of God in their lives, influences how they read and preach the text.[83] They seem more aware of this reality than other interpreters can be. Perhaps because we hear preachers, and as soon as we hear a preacher's voice, we are reminded of their particularity.[84] Our voices are distinctive; Turner and Hudson argue that our voice "symbolizes the self."[85] Zimmerman suggests evangelicals need to move past the unhelpful divide between objective and subjective knowledge and instead head towards understanding "truth as embodied."[86] Such a perspective allows us to escape homogeneity masked as objectivity.

Gadamer has also reminded me that each preacher is located "within traditions."[87] A preacher is always historically located and working in a tradition. Contrary to Enlightenment thought, tradition need not be bad or necessarily lead to relativism. For Gadamer, the fact that we can dialogue creates a "shared reality."[88] Indeed, it is impossible to separate oneself from a tradition. Individuals draw from and make contributions to the tradition in which they work. A good tradition is one where there is room for both criticism and creative thought.[89] Buttrick suggests that instead of a preacher asking, "What is the text saying to me?," which is the approach commonly taken, it would be more appropriate to interpret and preach conscious of the faith community and tradition in which they operate.[90] Such a view could change preaching from being an overly individualistic endeavor to a more collaborative process.[91] I am consciously working in

---

83. Quicke, *360-Degree Preaching*, 155.

84. Donovan Turner and Hudson, *Saved from Silence*, 10.

85. Donovan Turner and Hudson, *Saved from Silence*, 10.

86. Zimmermann, *Recovering Theological Hermeneutics*, 179.

87. Gadamer, *Truth and Method*, 294.

88. Grenz, *Primer on Postmodernism*, 110. In Gadamer's words the purpose of dialogue is reaching an understanding, "being transformed into a communion in which we do not remain what we were." See Gadamer, *Truth and Method*, 387.

89. Gadamer, *Truth and Method*, 293, 305; MacIntyre, *Whose Justice?*, 350; Mitchell, *Theological Ping-Pong*, 148. Sloane also addresses this in his analysis of Wolterstorff's ideas on control beliefs and how they work in a scholar's life and research. See Sloane, "Wolterstorff," 198–224.

90. Buttrick, *Homiletic*, 277.

91. Some thought has been given to collaborative preaching, but this is still an area that could be further reflected on. See McClure, *Roundtable Pulpit*.

the evangelical tradition, aiming to contribute to and challenge it. I am both an individual and a member of this community.

Gadamer draws on Heidegger's notion of the hermeneutical circle to argue that not only are we historically located, but even the very act of reading must balance understanding a particular part with understanding how it fits into the whole text. This tension can create initial impressions of a text that will have to be revised as we become aware of how our prejudices may distort our understanding.[92] Gadamer argues that when a person is aware of their bias, it allows them to be more open and come to the text ready to acknowledge its "otherness."[93] This is the stance I want to take as a preacher, as I look, like Gouldbourne says, "for the gracious action of God the Spirit to act within us and among us graciously, to transform us."[94] Texts are not just objects: people communicate through texts and make claims. A preacher's preunderstandings can be revised, leading to new interpretations.[95] With each reading of the text, our preunderstandings might change or be confirmed. One of the ways we can become aware of our prejudices is to hear from others.[96] This requires a preacher to be open to another person's ideas and aware of our thoughts and biases.[97] Gadamer uses the dialogue metaphor to describe how understanding is a back-and-forth process.[98] In fact, for Gadamer, this happens whenever we want to understand a text; we enter into a conversation, and a "fusion of horizons" happens as both an individual and the text interact.[99]

This idea of a dialogue can be supported at a theological level. The Bible models an open dialogue between God and humanity in the context of a covenant, including people bringing their "complaints, confusions and even occasional accusations" to God.[100] Through this wrestling, a deeper understanding of both God and people emerges. A preacher enters into

---

92. Gadamer, *Truth and Method*, 278–84. Gadamer draws on Schleiermacher's ideas of the hermeneutical circle. See Gadamer, *Truth and Method*, 302–10.

93. Gadamer, *Truth and Method*, 282.

94. Gouldbourne, "Embodied Voice."

95. Westphal, *Whose Community?*, 108; Wolterstorff, *Divine Discourse*, 54–57, 182.

96. Gadamer, *Truth and Method*, 310.

97. Gadamer, *Truth and Method*, 282.

98. Gadamer, *Truth and Method*, 376–77.

99. Gadamer, *Truth and Method*, 406.

100. Boyd, *Crucifixion*, 13; Reed, *Dialogues of the Word*, 36; Brueggemann, *Redescribing Reality*, 11.

a dialogue with a text, seeking to listen (with the help of the Spirit) to the author's intentions and to God's intentions. For evangelicals, this is not an equal partnership. Evangelical preachers are trying to submit to God as the final authority, with the biblical text functioning as the mediator of that authority.[101] Preachers need to recognize that they are finite human beings, not God. We should approach the Bible aware that each one of us is affected by sin; hence, preachers must be willing to submit their sermons to criticism.[102] After dialoguing with the text, a preacher shares this encounter with a group of listeners and continues the conversation by inviting them in turn to respond (and trusting the Spirit is also at work in them).[103] A preacher thus needs to be conscious of the text, their listeners, and themselves. What we bring to the Bible matters.

A significant question that lingers is how can a preacher know if their interpretation is getting closer to understanding the text or whether their reading is simply inadequate.[104] This is also a question that Habermas asks of Gadamer. Habermas critiques Gadamer and his reliance on tradition to distinguish how interpretations are judged.[105] Habermas argues that Gadamer downplays how ideology and power distort the traditions, making it harder for interpreters to communicate and know.[106] This tension between whether we can even speak about legitimate and non-legitimate understandings of a text and how we work it out will be answered differently depending on whether a preacher has a critical realist or anti-realist perspective.

Author, Text, and Preacher: A Critical Realist's Perspective

There is a close relationship between the author, text, and reader as they enter into dialogue with one another. How that works is contested. The emphasis in wider scholarship has shifted in recent times to expose the reader/

---

101. Doriani, *Putting Truth to Work*, 65.

102. Fowl, *Engaging Scripture*, 82. Also: Briggs, *Virtuous Reader*, 45–69.

103. Some evangelical preachers would be uncomfortable with this metaphor, fearful of the Bible becoming simply an "active participant." See Crotts, *Illuminated Preaching*, 40–43.

104. Osborne, *Hermeneutical Spiral*, 471.

105. Habermas, "Review," 236–38.

106. Habermas, "Review," 237–41.

preacher's role in the act of interpretation.[107] Some of this has been helpful. For instance, Derrida claims that nobody can ever exhaust all meaning from a particular story. He draws on a parable to argue that meaning is not stable or linked to the author's intentions, and efforts should be made to guard against any attempt to fix meaning. In the end, he states: "we are *before* this text," the text says "nothing definite" and presents "no identifiable content beyond the story itself, except for an endless *différance*."[108] Gadamer argues along similar lines, stating that the meaning of a text cannot be limited to either the author's original intentions nor how the original reader received the text because the very act of writing and passing on a text releases it, allowing "new relationships" to form.[109] Plato once lamented this fact: writing down an idea means it can easily fall "victim to misunderstanding" because the author is not there to aid those reading it.[110] However, deconstructionists tend to celebrate this ambiguity. A deconstructionist reads the text closely, looking for the unspoken tensions to unsettle "the established hierarchies of Western thought."[111] According to Derrida, the whole notion of truth and meaning is an illusion that often we (as preachers) have created and then guarded. Deconstructionist readers are much more suspicious of tradition and seek to unearth implicit presuppositions. For instance, Derrida points out how language is a human construction, which we treat as natural and universal.[112] Deconstructionist readers raise concerns that human beings cannot escape language nor reach the transcendent.

Foucault also attacks the notion that the "author" is vital in establishing meaning. He traces the history of the "author," arguing the importance of the author is linked to a particular discourse that developed alongside the rise in legal discourse and property rights.[113] He claims the notion of an "author" is used to limit and define texts and thus control meaning.[114] Again, this is perceived negatively by Foucault, particularly when such control leads to marginalization. This concern is also raised by liberation

---

107. McKnight, *Postmodern Use*. This in contrast to Schleiermacher, who sought to put the reader "'inside' the author." Schleiermacher and Kimmerle, *Hermeneutics*, 64.

108. Derrida, "Before the Law," 211.

109. Gadamer, *Truth and Method*, 413.

110. Gadamer, *Truth and Method*, 411.

111. Odell-Scott, "Deconstruction," 56.

112. Derrida, "Before the Law," 206.

113. Foucault, "What Is an Author?," 124.

114. Foucault, "What Is an Author?," 123.

hermeneutics.[115] Both Foucault and liberation scholars address how certain interpretive communities hold and maintain their power by claiming how they read and interpret is not only right but natural. These communities do so "in an attempt to constrain and determine what can and can't be thought" to perpetuate their power.[116] Deconstructionist readers seek to expose any ambiguities, unsolved struggles, and contradictions in a text that interpreters have overlooked or harmonized. Deconstructionists want to break down the dominance and authority of such interpretative communities.[117] Hence, they are suspicious of those who claim to explain a text definitively or try to find universal principles. Foucault raises awareness of the damage universal principles can do by erasing differences. He celebrates the specific.[118]

Evangelical preachers can learn from deconstructionists.[119] The critique deconstructionists make around power and interpretation is a valuable insight that evangelical preachers and churches must be aware of and address. The danger of claiming universal principles is also worth noting, as evangelicals can claim to be doing this when preaching. Some evangelicals acknowledge that "all texts have some degree of openness"; there are things left unsaid in a text while also recognizing there is much we can know.[120] A crucial difference between the deconstructionist thinker and an evangelical is their understanding of reality, whether it can ever be grasped and made known through language. Deconstructionists tend to take an anti-realist perspective, whereas I take a critical realist perspective.

An anti-realist stance would argue we can never reach "the real world"; such a notion is false, and there is no such thing.[121] Instead, we construct our perspective of the world through powerful illusions generated by language.[122] Derrida and others would assert that there is no transcendent truth and no way for the divine voice to speak to us. Lose does not deny

---

115. Stackhouse, *Need to Know*, 51.

116. Schirato and Yell, *Communication and Cultural Literacy*, 85.

117. Odell-Scott, "Deconstruction," 56.

118. Grenz, *Primer on Postmodernism*, 127.

119. Not all evangelicals would agree with this statement. Mathewson speaks about deconstructionism as a "bully" evangelical preachers must resist, see: Mathewson, *Art of Preaching*, 36.

120. Goldingay, *Models for Interpretation*, 51.

121. See key text: Nietzsche, *Will to Power*.

122. Grenz, *Primer on Postmodernism*, 91.

that our perspective of the world is always "mediated by discourse," but he goes on to say just because this is so does "not mean there is no such reality."[123] Although currently not fashionable, I take the position, along with Vanhoozer, that the person who creates a text wants to communicate, and those who read it can grasp this communication to some extent. This epistemological position is known as critical realism.[124] It acknowledges that every human being can both know and distort things, whether in acts of communication or knowledge of the world.[125]

An evangelical has certain theological presuppositions that under-pin a critical realist stance. For evangelicals, the remarkable claim that the Bible makes is that God became a particular individual; Jesus was bound in time and space so that human beings might approach and know this transcendent other. God works through a specific community, Israel, and specific texts to communicate. Vanhoozer argues that language is a gift by which we come to know others, including God.[126] He draws on Plantinga, who contends that humans "are constructed according to a certain design plan."[127] There is a reason and purpose for language. For Vanhoozer, lan-guage is "the medium of covenantal relations with God, others, and the world."[128] Given the complexity of reality, we try to understand and rep-resent reality in various forms, but we will never grasp it all.[129] A preacher can trust in God speaking and also recognize "that God's speech comes through human speech," which is fragile, incomplete, and distorted by sin.[130] This is to hold to a critical realist position.

A preacher wants to listen to both the human and divine author(s) because disregarding the author's claims in a text is seen as a form of abuse and manipulation; it is failing to let the "other" speak.[131] The very

123. Lose, *Confessing Jesus Christ*, 163.

124. Significant figures who in different ways argue this are: Vanhoozer, *Meaning*; Wright, *New Testament*, 32–80; Stackhouse, *Need to Know*; Patterson, *Realist Christian Theology*.

125. Sparks, *God's Word in Human Words*, 42–43.

126. Vanhoozer, *Meaning*, 205.

127. Plantinga, *Warrant and Proper Function*, 13.

128. Vanhoozer, *Meaning*, 206.

129. Stackhouse, *Need to Know*, 142.

130. Lose, *Confessing Jesus Christ*, 139.

131. Feminist homiletic scholar Florence says that the purpose of preaching is for the preacher to be convicted and "formed by the Other—or by the text." See Florence, *Preaching as Testimony*, 92.

purpose of language is for communication and understanding. There are tools and methods we have to be able to (mostly) understand one another. Webb suggests that it is possible to listen to a text because the reader recognizes the author's "scripted voice."[132] Hirsch, likewise, argues that a reader can understand an author's intentions through the text. He writes about how language imposes "an unavoidable limitation on the wills of both the author and interpreter."[133] Ricoeur agrees that while there is more than one meaning in a text, this does not mean anything goes because the "text presents a limited field of possible constructions."[134] He calls out the extreme of saying the author completely governs the meaning of the text, and we can completely know it, and the extreme of arguing that the text is wholly disconnected from the author.[135] If we read the Bible this way, we treat the text with respect like we would "a friend."[136] This often means that with ancient texts, there is a "measure of initial restraint."[137] Seitz says this means that, for instance, when we read the Old Testament, we need to read it "conscious of our place" outside ancient Israel.[138] We can allow the text to direct and question us.[139] An evangelical preacher seeks to listen as closely as possible to the biblical text.

The Bible Matters in Preaching

A Christian preacher believes that Yahweh communicates and that people bear God's image; likewise, we communicate.[140] Jesus, as found in the Bible, is believed to be good news worth announcing.[141] Homiletics is concerned with the oral communication of that gospel.[142] In the Scriptures, people hear

---

132. Webb, *Divine Voice*, 201.

133. Hirsch, *Validity in Interpretation*, 27.

134. Ricoeur, *Interpretation Theory*, 79. He also speaks about the surplus of meanings that arise in the use of language, particularly when using metaphors. See Ricoeur, *Interpretation Theory*, 45.

135. Ricoeur, *Interpretation Theory*, 30.

136. Webb, *Old Texts*, 26.

137. Biddle, *Reading Judges*, 5.

138. Seitz, *Elder Testament*, 56.

139. Webb, *Old Texts*, 26.

140. Gen 1:27; Gen 3. Also, Lee, *Preaching God's Grand Drama*, 22.

141. Millar and Campbell, *Saving Eutychus*, 77.

142. Chan, *Preaching*, 3.

the message of Jesus and then proclaim it.[143] A sermon is not just a lecture teaching people doctrines about God but seeks to be a place where people "encounter God."[144] This means, says Gross, that hermeneutics is essential to preaching.[145] The Bible is important to evangelicals. It follows that interpretation also matters. There are many metaphors given for this task. Different people will identify more with one than another, but one of the metaphors that has shaped me is that of a storyteller.[146] Storytellers in preaching are "poets charged with the task of keeping and imparting the stories" of God.[147] My first degree was in media production. I have always been interested in the power of stories. My passion is communicating the gospel so people can participate in God's story. As I will discuss in future chapters, this view of the preacher impacts how I approach sermons.

Evangelicals tend to emphasise the importance of expository preaching. According to Kaiser, an expository sermon "allows the biblical text to supply both the shape and content of the message."[148] Gross writes about the impact of the "new hermeneutic" in helping preachers identify the need for a "double awareness": holding the text's historical context and the current context in which the text is preached in tension.[149] She describes biblical preaching as an "encounter with the text" in order to encounter Christ.[150] Lose contends that when a preacher operates in a dialogical framework, they will be moved to speak but do so aware of their cultural location and, therefore, will preach with "integrity and responsibility," acknowledging that their preaching is "provisional" and sits within a wider dialogue.[151] This understanding of preaching presents a more dynamic process between the preacher and the text. Buttrick adds that preaching should search for "the mystery of Jesus Christ crucified through scripture."[152] When this hap-

---

143. Acts 5:42; Col 1:23–28; 1 John 1:3.

144. Capill, *Heart Is the Target*, 17.

145. Gross, *Cannot Preach*, 91.

146. Williams, "Preaching as Storytelling," 121.

147. Arthur, *God-Hungry Imagination*, 31.

148. Kaiser, *Preaching and Teaching*, 49. See also: Millar and Campbell, *Saving Eutychus*, 30–31.

149. Gross, *Cannot Preach*, 72.

150. Gross, *Cannot Preach*, 89.

151. Lose, *Confessing Jesus Christ*, 60.

152. Buttrick, *Homiletic*, 249.

pens, it can be said that the preacher has spoken the very word of God.[153] When someone preaches, they necessarily believe that "God uses the utterly frail and human speech of his witnesses, including those of preachers" to address people.[154] The hope is that one person can speak to a whole group, and that group will grasp their message more or less.

According to Thompson, an evangelical preacher should have a relationship with God, having received the grace God offers in Jesus Christ.[155] Kay brings together the two concepts of God as the "ultimate Agent of preaching" and the person who is preaching.[156] When a preacher communicates the Bible to others, the belief is that the Spirit works through the preacher and those listening.[157] When God's Word and Spirit are at work, "the living God speaks" through the preacher.[158] Preaching is "a conversation initiated by God" that ideally is designed to lead people to worship the Triune God in all aspects of their lives.[159] The sermon in most evangelical churches has a central place in the Sunday worship gatherings. The desire to apply the Bible concretely to our listeners should be at the heart of a sermon.

Application Is Part of the Reading Process

Application is concerned with connecting the biblical text to the contemporary context. It is focused on the question: why does this ancient text matter now? Though critical in the interpretative process, application is often under-thought.[160] Schleiermacher was one of the first scholars to treat hermeneutics as a science, whereby the interpreter aimed to reverse the process of grammar and composition to determine the meaning.[161] One

153. The Reformed tradition, including influential figures such as Luther, Calvin, and Barth, has long championed this view. See Chan, *Preaching*, 13.

154. Kay, *Preaching and Theology*, 19.

155. Thompson, *Preaching Biblically*, 44.

156. Kay, *Preaching and Theology*, 5.

157. Goldsworthy, *Preaching the Whole Bible*, 85; Heisler, *Spirit-Led Preaching*, 19.

158. Johnson, *Glory of Preaching*, 32.

159. Paquarello, *Christian Preaching*, 31.

160. It is discussed at a popular academic level. See Doriani, *Putting Truth to Work*. Osborne also has two chapters discussing the relationship between interpretation and application. See Osborne, *Hermeneutical Spiral*. See also Foskett, *Interpreting the Bible*. Gadamer also refers to this problem in Gadamer, *Truth and Method*, 318.

161. Schleiermacher and Kimmerle, *Hermeneutics*, 62.

of the results of his work was to separate interpretation from application—or, as some scholars call it, "meaning" from "significance."[162] This leads to a two-step process. Stott uses the metaphor of a chasm to describe the gap between the meaning of the text and its application.[163] Homiletical texts tend to address application but fail to connect these discussions to the wider hermeneutical conversation. Similarly, many biblical commentaries have little to say by way of application.[164] This is unsatisfactory because it creates the impression that exegesis and application are two unrelated components of a sermon. In reality, it is hard to split exegesis and application neatly.[165] Indeed, Capill argues that when it comes to a sermon, "biblical exposition itself must be applicatory."[166] When preachers understand the text, they simultaneously apply it to their context.[167] This is why preachers need to know how they are reading the Bible.

Gadamer draws on preaching to argue that interpretation and application work together.[168] Preaching unlocks the dynamics of interpretation.[169] Gadamer argues that this is the interpreter's job: to apply the text to the current historical situation.[170] Homiletical texts use similar language, with Quicke saying that the preacher must be "alert to the responses that God is calling" for in a particular time, place, and people.[171] This diversity creates "differences over the way a story applies to different people."[172] Application aims to show how a biblical text is relevant to those listening; it

162. Wright, *New Testament*, 23; Gross, *Cannot Preach*, 75; Osborne, *Hermeneutical Spiral*, 410.

163. Stott, *Between Two Worlds*, 137–79. According to Gross this became the dominant metaphor, see Gross, *Cannot Preach*, 76.

164. Gignilliat and Pennington trace this change arguing that it was in modernity that this separation developed when academic commentaries came to mean "somehow objective and nonpersonal, nonsapiential, and nonexhortational" compared to application. See Gignilliat and Pennington, "Theological Commentary," 239–40.

165. Doriani notes that the traditional view saw application as the last step in the process; first comes the exegesis, then the application. See Doriani, *Putting Truth to Work*, 18.

166. Capill, *Heart Is the Target*, 19.

167. Brown, *Holy Spirit*.

168. Wright, *New Testament*, 28. Ricoeur agrees with Gadamer that application is not "a contingent appendix added onto understanding." See Ricoeur, "World of the Text," 14.

169. Wright, *New Testament*, 29.

170. Gadamer, *Truth and Method*, 318.

171. Quicke, *360-Degree Preaching*, 154.

172. Goldingay, *Models for Interpretation*, 53.

places the gospel in real "lived experience."[173] The preacher tries to connect the text to those listening so they recognize they are hearing God's Word and are moved to respond in some way.[174] Holt and Spears argue that the "primary context" for the Bible is the church that has been formed and summoned to listen to God's voice; as the church listens, God's purposes are applied and lived out.[175] Hermeneutics and homiletics, therefore, need to work in partnership. There are two prevalent evangelical approaches to forming application. While these approaches are common and have some merit, I find both approaches unsatisfactory. Instead, I propose that when developing application, we need to consider the role of the preacher, the role of the listener, and the role of the text. When all three align, then we have application that will powerfully resonate.

Approach 1: Principles

A popular approach among evangelicals is to determine the underlying principle of the biblical text before applying that principle to the current context. In this approach, you can follow a series of rules to understand a text's meaning and application. The aim is to get to the "timeless truth."[176] First, the preacher grasps the authorial intention and then summarizes that intention into a "single proposition."[177] This is also known as the "big idea."[178] Then comes application, and application clearly "rests" upon exegesis.[179] The function of the application is to describe "the intended effects of the truth" found in Scripture.[180] According to Kuhatschek, this works by applying the principle to an identical situation in our context or to a comparable situation.[181] Murray adds that the focus of application

173. Webb, *Old Texts*, 36; Thompson, *Preaching Biblically*, 51. Capill describes it as pressing the biblical truth onto the lives of our listeners. See Capill, *Heart Is the Target*, 30. Broadus defines application as when a preacher shows "how the subject applies to the person addressed." See Broadus, *Preparation and Delivery*, 211; Buttrick, *Homiletic*, 33.

174. Ortberg, "Biblical Preaching," 452.

175. Holt and Spears, "Ecclesia as Primary Context," 72–73.

176. Capill, *Heart Is the Target*, 47.

177. Arthurs, "Fundamentals of Sermon Application (Part 2)," 73. Also: Robinson, *Biblical Preaching*, 121; Stott, *Between Two Worlds*, 224.

178. Millar and Campbell, *Saving Eutychus*, 74; Murray, *How Sermons Work*, 110.

179. Doriani, *Putting Truth to Work*, 19. Also: Helm, "Idea of Inerrancy."

180. Doriani, *Putting Truth to Work*, 19.

181. Kuhatschek, *Guesswork*, 68. See also Stein, *Basic Guide*, 33; Larsen, *Anatomy of*

is not on the "accidental" or minor parts of the text but the core.[182] This sounds very straightforward.

However, such an approach rests on the assumption that a clear principle can be drawn from the text and that determining it is the goal of exegesis. This might work well for the letters in the New Testament, but it is not equally applicable to all biblical genres. For instance, Goldingay argues that for narratives, "the meaning of a story cannot really be abstracted from the story itself."[183] Brown notes that a theological point is frequently extracted from the text and turned into a timeless principle; thus, the conversation is reduced to determining what parts of the Bible are culturally bound and what timeless principles preachers can apply today.[184] This runs the risk of missing what is happening in a biblical text and presuming that we can extract timeless principles even though we are culturally bound.[185] Another critique from Gadamer, noted above, is that interpretation and application are not so neatly separated in practice. This approach does not adequately acknowledge the role of the preacher and the listener in shaping application. It assumes the preacher can easily extract and pluck out the principle and then apply it to our context without anything changing in that process. I find this approach to application to be of limited use and potentially dangerous because the preacher tends to deny or ignore their role in the interpretative process.

Approach 2: Speech Act Theory

A second approach to application that evangelicals have started to explore is connected to speech act theory. Authors use language not simply to state content but "to do things," and then the reader is invited to respond.[186] Speech act theory breaks the act of speech into three parts: the locutionary act (when we say something), the illocutionary act (what we do when saying something), and the perlocutionary act (the effect of the two previous

---

Preaching, 98; Kaiser Jr., *Preaching and Teaching*, 188.

182. Murray, *How Sermons Work*, 110.

183. Goldingay, *Models for Interpretation*, 52.

184. Brown, *Holy Spirit*, 261.

185. Brown, *Holy Spirit*, 262. Gross argues that this method actually puts the preacher "in complete charge" as they determine and search "for the true idea." See Gross, *Cannot Preach*, 79.

186. Kuruvilla, *Manual for Preaching*, 28.

acts on others).[187] It pays special attention to how these three parts work in a text.[188] The biblical text always has a message (locution) for the preacher; that message has a "force" to it that "aims to affect the hearer" (illocution), which may produce a "response from the hearer" (perlocution).[189] Speech act theory reminds people that the Bible is an act of communication. Fundamental to evangelicals' understanding of Scripture is that through it, God speaks to fulfill God's missional purposes.[190] The Bible is God's speech act that changes things; Kay says, "God's Word creates, institutes, and accomplishes a new state of affairs."[191] When preachers speak from God's Word, they join in creating something new. Thus, when applying the text, the preacher needs to consider the locution and illocutionary force and then consider both in the sermon.[192]

Other homileticians argue along similar lines without drawing explicitly from speech act theory. Craddock, for example, says that the sermon needs to both express the content of the biblical text and capture the function. This will affect how the application will be expressed.[193] Long has been enormously influential in my sermon processes. He writes that the literary form of a biblical text should shape the form of a sermon.[194] It is not just about plucking the principle out of the text but allowing the whole text to impact the congregation. This means being aware of the literary form when considering a sermon's application.[195] Speech act theory builds on that idea by also paying attention to the rhetoric of a text. Long sees the sermon as trying to "extend a portion of the text's impact into a new communicational situation," but only a portion, because he does not believe a sermon can grasp all the text is doing.[196] Gadamer would agree and argue that all interpretation is "highlighting," producing both a "clearer and flatter" product than the original.[197] Preachers often recognize they cannot say or do every-

---

187. Briggs, *Words in Action*, 40–41.

188. Briggs, *Words in Action*, 40–41.

189. Chan, *Preaching*, 213.

190. Stackhouse, *Need to Know*, 123.

191. Kay, *Preaching and Theology*, 11.

192. Chan, *Preaching*, 200.

193. Craddock, *Preaching*, 123.

194. Long, *Literary Forms*, 11.

195. Long, *Literary Forms*, 13.

196. Long, *Literary Forms*, 33.

197. Gadamer, *Truth and Method*, 404.

thing a biblical text could say and do. When a preacher limits what they are trying to say, the communication can be sharper and more appropriate to those they are addressing.[198] This approach encourages preachers to be aware of what the text is saying and how it is saying it.

Speech act theory has contributed to evangelicals' understanding of application. Of course, it does have weaknesses. According to Kuruvilla, discovering what an author is doing is difficult since this area lacks resources and is "more art than science, less amenable to being codified into steps."[199] The illocutionary force of the sermon would need to have the same or similar effect as the illocution in the original context.[200] This raises questions about how we navigate the fact that the context and listeners change over time. Again, the emphasis here is still primarily on the biblical text, with little awareness of the role of the preacher and the listener in the interpretative process. I want to take this approach and expand it slightly to include these two aspects.

Approach 3: Text, Preacher, and Listener

Considering the reflections on these two common evangelical approaches to application, I propose that a sermon is a dialogue between the biblical text, the preacher, and a particular congregation at a certain time and place.[201] There is something very elusive about application. This is because to understand and apply a text requires more than reason and careful methods. Capill describes a preacher's life and the text as "rubbing metal against metal," resulting in "richer life application."[202] This requires a preacher to listen and ask questions of the text and also to allow the text to challenge the preacher.[203] This means paying attention to the content and form of the biblical text, as suggested above, but also to

---

198. Craddock, *Preaching*, 156.

199. Kuruvilla, *Manual for Preaching*, 37. Kuruvilla does not think this is necessarily a bad thing. Gadamer would agree. He writes about play as an appropriate interpretive virtue that exegetes need to embrace more. See Gadamer, *Truth and Method*, 106–14.

200. Brown, *Holy Spirit*, 268.

201. Capill also uses the language of dialogue to describe the relationship between the text and the listeners. See Capill, *Heart Is the Target*, 50. See also Steimle et al., *Preaching the Story*.

202. Capill, *Heart Is the Target*, 93.

203. Brown, "Preacher as Interpreter," 105.

the preacher's context. Stackhouse speaks about the important role that intuition and imagination play.[204] Likewise, Kahneman talks about how "valid intuitions" develop when people become experts in their field and learn to "recognize familiar elements in a new situation."[205] A crucial role of the preacher is to have imagination.[206]

Brown describes preachers as needing to "enter into dialogue with a text on behalf of the congregation."[207] Such dialogue is fundamental to homiletics, as preaching begins with the God who first speaks.[208] When God speaks, there is new life and transformation. Human beings are invited to listen to God and then talk.[209] A dialogical perspective suggests that preaching and "listening is an ongoing, active, dynamic process."[210] How the preacher and the congregation respond to the biblical text is essential.[211] It is a task we must continue to reflect on and hone our skills in. As many homiletic texts note, preachers must reflect on their lives, observe people and culture, and read widely.[212] Ultimately, it is not just the preacher who judges whether an application has worked. Listeners need to be involved and ask themselves whether what they hear seems to be grounded in the text and their lived experiences. Does it resonate? The two application theories above have emphasized the text. Doriani counters this by arguing that preachers need to focus on those listening to the same extent as they are focused on the text. He suggests four questions that can lead to application: What is the text calling us to do? Who is it calling us to be? What should we be pursuing in life? How do we gain discernment?[213] There are a few homiletical texts that help evangelicals to think about their listeners. However, there is room for more work in this space.[214] There are also few evangelical homiletical books that discuss

204. Stackhouse, *Need to Know*, 127–34.

205. Kahneman, *Thinking, Fast and Slow*, 12.

206. Stackhouse, *Need to Know*, 133.

207. Brown, "Preacher as Interpreter," 105. Gross also proposes a dialogical method to preaching in her work. See Gross, *Cannot Preach*, 106–34.

208. Donovan Turner and Hudson, *Saved from Silence*, 17.

209. Donovan Turner and Hudson, *Saved from Silence*, 17.

210. Lose, *Confessing Jesus Christ*, 60.

211. Stein, *Basic Guide*, 38.

212. Capill, *Heart Is the Target*, 92.

213. Doriani, *Putting Truth to Work*, 98.

214. For example: Johnston, *Preaching to a Postmodern World*; Jeter Jr. and Allen, *One Gospel*; Long, "Taking the Listeners Seriously"; Robinson, "Listening to the Listeners."

feminist contributions. Doriani does try. He critiques feminism for its low view of scriptural authority.[215] Yet he also acknowledges a preacher needs to dialogue with people they might disagree with to understand their culture and apply the Bible to the contemporary context.[216]

Like Gadamer, I do not think application can be neatly locked away from interpretation. Therefore, when exploring how to preach, I will consider the sermon from three angles: the preacher, the listeners, and the text. Doriani proposes something similar, suggesting that application needs three elements: text, interpreter, and audience.[217] This approach acknowledges that meaning (which encompasses exegesis and application) arises in relationship with the author, the text, and the reader—and, for preachers, the extra dimension of the listener(s).

The Book of Judges

To show how this works, I am taking the book of Judges as a case study and working through some of my decisions as a preacher. I will be learning from feminists along the way. When it comes to understanding the book of Judges, there is a whole body of literature written from a range of perspectives that an evangelical preacher could draw from.[218] I will concentrate on selected works from evangelical and feminist scholarship.[219] Evangelicals are primarily interested in the theological implications of the text. There are many evangelical commentaries on the book of Judges. A few are explicitly aimed at preachers.[220] However, they tend to be less academic and rigorous in their exegesis.

---

215. Doriani, *Putting Truth to Work*, 34.

216. Doriani, *Putting Truth to Work*, 36–37.

217. Doriani, *Putting Truth to Work*, 35.

218. This is not meant to be an exhaustive list but to highlight the major scholarly works on the book of Judges: Boling, *Judges*; Brensinger, *Judges*; Brettler, *Book of Judges*; Butler, *Judges*; Chisholm Jr., *Commentary*; Conway, *Judging the Judges*; Erickson, "Judges"; Faley, *Joshua, Judges*; Frolov, *Judges*; Gunn, *Judges*; Hamlin, *At Risk*; Martin, *Book of Judges*; Matthews, *Judges and Ruth*; O'Connell, *Rhetoric*; Ryan, *Judges*; Sasson, *Judges 1–12*; Soggin, *Judges*; Way, *Judges and Ruth*.

219. Key evangelical commentaries include: Beldman, *Judges*; Block, *Judges, Ruth*; Boda and Schwab, *Judges, Ruth*; Cundall and Morris, *Judges*; Davis, *Judges*; Evans, *Judges and Ruth*; Webb, *Book of Judges*; Wilcock, *Message of Judges*.

220. Jeter Jr., *Preaching Judges*; McCann, *Judges*; Webb, *Judges and Ruth*; Younger Jr., *Judges and Ruth*.

Feminist scholarship is also quite broad—ranging from works in my tradition (evangelical egalitarian) to works with radically different presuppositions. Many feminist scholars have described the book of Judges as a "world of men's concerns, primarily war and occupation."[221] For this book, I have loosely divided feminist scholarship into three categories. Some works seek to be both evangelical/Christian and feminist. Then, there are works by scholars who are more critical of the biblical text but still give it some authority. Lastly, some feminists are reluctant to give any authority to the Bible. This latter group I call non-evangelical feminists, and they are the ones I have tried to engage with. Many non-evangelical feminist scholars have interpreted the book of Judges, including Bal, Brenner, Exum, Fuchs, Klein, and Yee.[222] Though difficult, I believe learning from people with radically different presuppositions to mine is a fruitful endeavor. These scholars have challenged my reading of the biblical text and opened my eyes to things I have missed. There seems to be little written combining non-evangelical feminist scholarship with evangelical homiletical scholarship. This is the gap I am seeking to fill.

It Matters How We Read the Bible

Preachers need to understand what presuppositions we bring to the biblical text. I have situated myself in this hermeneutical discussion and defended why I think it is reasonable for an evangelical to be a critical realist. I have also examined what this means for evangelical preaching. I have realized that a preacher needs to consider three key areas when shaping a sermon. First, they need to be aware of their role in the interpretive process. Second, evangelical preachers are focused on understanding the biblical text. They try to discern what the text is saying in both the original and contemporary context. Third, preachers must consider how those listening to a sermon will interact with the text as it is mediated through the preacher. I will be using this framework as I listen to feminist scholars work through some of the stories that feature women found in the book of Judges.

221. Klein, "Achsah," 19.

222. Bal, *Death and Dissymmetry* and *Murder and Difference*; Brenner, "Triangle and a Rhombus" and *Feminist Companion to Judges* and *to the Bible*; Exum, "On Judges 11" and "Feminist Criticism"; Fuchs, *Feminist Theory*; Klein, *Triumph of Irony*; Brenner and Yee, eds., *Joshua and Judges*.

Discussion Questions

Would you describe your preaching models and theological training as narrow or broad?

Who are you? What has shaped you? What traditions?

Listening to different voices will help a preacher become aware of the possible reactions people in their congregation might have to a text. How do you listen to other voices?

Exercise

Read through the whole book of Judges and keep a notebook with you. Jot down your initial responses. How do you feel as you read this? Write down any images, stories, feelings, questions, or experiences that come to mind. You might also want to consider how you would divide this book into a preaching series. How many weeks would you like to spend on this book? What stories would you like to focus on? Are there any stories you wouldn't want to address?

2

Why preach a first-person narrative?

AS A FEMALE PREACHER, I often felt my voice was not as important or valued as others. For a long time, I was nervous every time I preached. My throat would go dry, and my face would turn bright red. So, to discover my voice, I started engaging with the feminist scholar Mieke Bal. Bal wrote a series of books focused on Judges in the 1980s.[1] Bal approaches the Bible conscious that she is a Dutch secular cultural theorist and critic. She reads the Bible within that academic tradition. Indeed, her works are quite academic. The Bible is worth studying for Bal because it "has been formative [in] Western culture."[2] She does not read the Bible for "moral, religious, or political" instruction.[3] Instead, Bal wants to know how gender is constructed through these texts. She states that her intended audience is those concerned about "the history of gender-relations" and those who want to explore the tensions of working with historical documents.[4]

1. When these books were written Bal was a professor of semiotics and women's studies at Utrecht University, however, she took time off from Utrecht to write *Death and Dissymmetry*. Bal notes that she wrote *Death and Dissymmetry* at the Harvard Divinity School while she was a fellow in the women's studies in religion program. By the time of publication, she also occupied a position at the University of Rochester in the US. *Murder and Difference* was published and translated into English by Matthew Gumpert in 1988. Bal oversaw the process, finalizing the book, while also working on *Death and Dissymmetry*, also published in 1988.

2. Bal, "Introduction," 11.

3. Bal, *Lethal Love*, 1.

4. Bal, *Death and Dissymmetry*, 3.

This makes her work quite niche. Bal presupposes that the book of Judges is a literary work with some connection to historical reality which the text "both hide(s) and display(s)."[5] Yet even more crucial for Bal is how the reader approaches the text. Bal seeks to make people conscious of the dominant readings of Judges by offering a counter-reading. Her reading challenges both what the story of Judges is about and deeper still challenges the notion of a fixed single meaning in a text.

Bal calls her reading approach "counter-coherence."[6] This form of deconstruction leads her to argue that the book of Judges is less about politics and war and more about a "social revolution that concerns the institution of marriage."[7] While I don't agree with all her conclusions, she did get me thinking about what this approach could mean for preachers. Bal states that her research is interdisciplinary work that draws from a range of sources. She argues in *Murder and Difference* that a multidisciplinary perspective is critical for it helps a reader "liberate ourselves from the restrictions" that one code/method might bring.[8] Bal covers many methods, but in particular, she uses narrative theory, women's studies, and psychoanalytic interpretation.[9] Drawing from these theoretical frameworks, she operates with certain checks and balances.[10] These theories are equal to the biblical text and brought into a "dialogue" in order "to learn something from the encounter: to change."[11]

I want to apply this reading strategy to preaching.[12] Bal demonstrates that whenever someone reads, they form a story or coherence. People like unity.[13] In recent decades, there has been an increased appreciation for the power of stories and a fresh realization that the Bible tells a story about God.[14] Bal picks up this interest in narratives by interrogating whose voice tells us the story and whose voice never speaks. Using a counter-coherence

5. Bal, *Death and Dissymmetry*, 3.

6. Bal, *Death and Dissymmetry*, 5.

7. Bal, *Death and Dissymmetry*, 5.

8. Bal, *Murder and Difference*, 136–37.

9. Bal, *Death and Dissymmetry*, 6–7.

10. Bal, *Death and Dissymmetry*, 6.

11. Bal, "Dealing/with/Women," 317.

12. Bal, *Death and Dissymmetry*.

13. In traditional homiletical theory, preachers are encouraged to have one central idea that will give "coherence and direction to the shape the sermon takes." See Rose, *Sharing the Word*, 18.

14. Bausch, *Storytelling*, 15–28.

approach, an evangelical preacher could deliberately choose to identify with a minor character in the biblical narrative and amplify that voice.[15] First-person narrative sermons can be used for this exact purpose. It is worth considering why a preacher might use a certain sermonic structure. Often, homiletical books focus on giving practical instructions. For instance, there are many works on how to preach a first-person narrative sermon, but not many explain why you might use this particular structure.[16] Bal reminds us the story you tell matters. By exploring Bal's work, I will state the case for why first-person narrative sermons, particularly those that focus on minor characters, matter. Achsah's story in Judges 1 will be our case study.

Counter-Coherence and the Preacher

A counter-coherence approach, by its very definition, is about telling an alternate story. Bal's reading is an act of resistance. She takes the textual elements from the book of Judges, particularly the minor elements, and asks whether they can be arranged in another way to produce a new story.[17] This story is still grounded in the text but focuses on the ignored or neglected aspects. Now, this can make some evangelical preachers uncomfortable. Evangelical preachers typically want to determine the author's intention and can be wary about concentrating on the margins. However, many evangelical preachers also recognize that a text can have more than one fixed meaning.[18] After all, evangelical preachers read Old Testament texts in light of Jesus Christ; the gospel sheds new understanding onto older texts.[19] As an egalitarian evangelical preacher, I see Jesus valuing minor voices, particularly women, and this informs how I read the Old Testament texts. An evangelical preacher can, therefore, resist not the biblical text *per se* but certain standard interpretations. A counter-coherence approach can help me see things I might otherwise miss.[20]

15. Durber, another preacher learning from feminist scholars, also suggests this approach: Durber, *Preaching Like a Woman*, 26.

16. See Robinson and Robinson, *It's All in How You Tell It*; Garner, *Getting into Character*; Edwards, *Effective First-Person Biblical Preaching*.

17. Bal, *Death and Dissymmetry*, 2–5.

18. Goldsworthy, *Gospel-Centred Hermeneutics*, 205.

19. Enns, *Inspiration and Incarnation*, 154.

20. When you start investigating you see a concern for marginal people throughout the Scriptures. For instance, the book of Ruth and the story of Hannah in 1 Samuel 1–2

What motivates resistance depends on the preacher, which is precisely Bal's contention. Preachers desire some form of coherence: the aim is often to have unity between the text and the application of that text in our present context.[21] Bal proposes that a preacher's choices when interpreting a text are driven by their interests. It comes down to an understanding of a preacher's authority and power.[22] In Bal's counter-coherence approach, she gives a narratological analysis of the text. She asks who is the subject in this text and what role they play.[23] In other words, who gets to speak, and what authority do they have? These are also crucial questions for preachers.

Female preachers in evangelical circles are in the minority in Sydney. In many evangelical churches, the main person who preaches every week is male. The identity of the speaker matters. Even if a church allows women to preach, the next question that needs to be asked is: how often do they speak? The website "Fixing Her Eyes" has tried to create an Australian map listing which churches have female preachers; it looks encouraging at first glance.[24] But the criteria are quite broad. The list makes no distinction between churches where a woman occasionally speaks and churches where women preach regularly.

A limited sense of power and authority is given when women are only occasionally allowed to speak. Yet, from that position, there is the opportunity to become a counter-voice. Such a preacher can become prophetic and offer a different perspective.[25] Though this is not the ideal situation (I would love to see a more equal representation of women and men speaking), for those who work in such a reality, reframing their purpose might be useful.[26] Who speaks and how much power they have will impact how they speak, understand the text, and apply it. This applies, of course, not just to women but to other marginalized groups. A preacher can ask the question that Bal

---

explore how God works through women in vulnerable positions. And the story of Rachel is picked up in Jeremiah 31:5 and Matthew 2:18 as a lament calling out to God to come and save.

21. Chapell, *Christ-Centered Sermons*, 210.

22. Allen, *Preaching and the Other*, 57.

23. Bal, *Death and Dissymmetry*, appendix 1.

24. "Churches Where Women Preach in Australia."

25. Other feminist scholars such as Anna Carter Florence also make this point. Florence argues that "women proclaim scripture through a hermeneutics of marginality." See Florence, *Preaching as Testimony*, 96.

26. Florence argues that in fact there is greater authority in preaching when you are powerless. Florence, *Preaching as Testimony*, 103.

herself raises: Who do we identify with in the narrative? She argues that the narrator identifies with the male characters.[27] For example, in Judges 1, a woman is present: Achsah briefly appears, but the focus is on Othniel and Caleb.[28] As noted in the introduction, the book of Judges focuses on men and the stories they want to tell. If a preacher is trying to follow the author's intentions, then a preacher would tend to focus on the male characters and perspectives.[29] Feminist scholars argue that what it means to be human is usually read and understood through what it means to be male. Even female preachers, especially those working within the evangelical tradition, can absorb this androcentric perspective.[30] It becomes normalized.

With a counter-coherence approach, an evangelical preacher would deliberately identify with a minor character in the biblical narrative and sit with that character.[31] They could utilize Bal's strategy and focus on a text's marginal elements. A preacher must use their imagination as a key "interpretive tool."[32] Imagination is one of the ways we come to know and understand things.[33] First-person narratives are a powerful way to do this. First-person narratives are not a new concept, but Bal's counter-coherence approach helps explain why first-person narratives can be so moving. In my sermon, I wanted to highlight the voice of Achsah. What questions might she have about God? A preacher can identify with those who are powerless and feel what it might be like to be in a similar position.

I found it hard at first to find Achsah's voice. I would have skipped over her if I wasn't looking for women in the text. Judges 1 opens by setting the scene of what life is like in Israel after Joshua's death. Israel is looking for the next man or men to lead them into battle as they seek to finish claiming the land of Canaan, which Yahweh has given as an inheritance to them. Caleb, a contemporary of Joshua and the only other of the twelve spies who argued they should take the land Yahweh had given them back in Numbers 13, appears in Judges 1, leading the charge against the Canaanites. In Judges 1:12, he offers his daughter, Achsah, to the man who will lead the army and capture the city of Debir. In the next verse, we are introduced to Othniel,

27. Bal, *Death and Dissymmetry*, 235.

28. Ratner, "Playing Fathers' Games," 148.

29. Cheney also addresses this in her work, *She Can Read*.

30. Brenner and van Dijk Hemmes, *On Gendering Texts*, 21.

31. Durber also suggests this approach in her *Preaching Like a Woman*, 26.

32. Robinson and Robinson, *It's All in How You Tell It*, 13.

33. Stackhouse, *Need to Know*, 131–34.

Caleb's relative. He takes up the offer, conquers the city, and is given Achsah in marriage. The story lingers as we listen to Achsah's conversation with Othniel. In verse 14, she urges her husband to ask her father for a lush field. But instead of Othniel, Achsah approaches her father and asks for a better inheritance. He grants her request, and the story moves on away from her. Othniel appears briefly in Judges 3, where he is described as a good judge, filled with the Spirit of God, delivering Israel and bringing peace.

There is so little information given in the text about Achsah. It was only by reading a wide range of feminist scholars that I began to find my way into Achsah's story. Fewell's words, in particular, provoked my interest. She noted that the city mentioned in Judges 1:11 was originally named Kiriath-sepher, meaning "the city of writing" or the "city of books."[34] The Israelites change its name, and by doing so, Fewell says they sought to soften the fact that a city of knowledge and culture is "simply erased."[35] This is what happens to women as well in the book of Judges. They are marginalized or erased.[36] Christians often treat the book of Judges as a historical account outlining the early days of Israelite settlement, which means that this portrayal of women can be taken as normative and neutral.[37] In the sermon, I decided to explore the erasure of people and places in the stories we create and pass on as Scripture. I believe that all voices are part of God's story and have something to teach us about ourselves and God. One of the benefits of preaching a first-person narrative sermon is the chance to listen to and amplify a single voice. A preacher cannot say everything about a text, but focusing on one of the marginal voices present in the text can help those listening to hear something from God they have not heard before.

Achsah: The Biblical Text

A counter-coherence sermon focuses on aspects of the biblical text that tend to be neglected or ignored to tell a story. Many scholars speak about the narrative shape of the Bible: it both tells one overarching story and is a collection of stories.[38] Smith notes that feminist scholars often expose the negative

34. Fewell, "Deconstructive Criticism," 125.

35. Fewell, "Deconstructive Criticism," 125.

36. Fuchs, *Sexual Politics*, 11.

37. Fuchs, *Sexual Politics*, 12.

38. Allen, "Theology Undergirding Narrative Preaching," 33.

portrayals of women.[39] However, the feminist scholars who have examined Achsah's short story are divided as to how she should be understood. Even in a few brief verses, a complex, ambiguous character emerges. Achsah is introduced in verse 12 by her father, Caleb, who offers her as a prize to the man who captures the city of Kiriath-sepher. Many people today will find this jarring, though evangelical scholars, like Block, stress this would not have been shocking to the original hearers, and indeed, Achsah may well have been "honored to be given in marriage to a military hero like Othniel."[40] I raise this as a possibility in the sermon:

> Some of the other girls were jealous. There were lots of daydreams, lots of talk about who were the greatest warriors, the emerging heroes of our generation. We were waiting, wanting to be married. We thought that's when life really started. I think I was excited, or maybe I was scared.

Some evangelicals celebrate her as a role model for other women.[41] A sign that women are valued and have an important place in Israelite society. The other possibility is that Achsah's story is reinforcing the patriarchal system. Klein describes her as representative of all Israelite women, both "valued and a passive object."[42] In verse 14, Achsah is given some agency. She approaches Othniel. Klein sees her using her sexuality to assert herself, arguing that the phrase "she came" in verse 14 suggests she approached Othniel once he was sexually satisfied.[43] She becomes a paradigm for other wives wanting to "influence their all-powerful husbands by using their sexuality."[44] Again, I tried to put this possibility out there, so I tell Achsah's story in three different ways:

> At least that's how my husband tells the story. He loves telling the story at night when I am wrapped up in his arms. His deep voice rumbles. He says I seduced him, removing my veil, eager for him to touch me and be with me. And then afterward, when he's all smiling and satisfied, I convinced him we should approach my father and ask for land, good land. Sometimes, when he tells the story, it changes slightly, and he says it took many nights of me speaking

39. Smith, "Delilah," 105.
40. Block, *Judges, Ruth*, 94.
41. Block, *Judges, Ruth*, 95; Evans, *Judges and Ruth*, 43–44.
42. Klein, "Paradigm and Deviation," 56.
43. Klein, "Paradigm and Deviation," 57.
44. Klein, "Paradigm and Deviation," 58.

about it, and he got so tired of my nagging that he gave in. Once,
when he told the story to others, he said it was his idea from the
beginning. It's a delicate balance communicating with your husband,
don't you think?

In the end, though, Achsah rather than her husband approaches her
father. We are not told why she goes instead of Othniel. Bal argues that
Achsah is quite assertive, particularly when she approaches her father. She
pictures Achsah clapping her hands at Caleb to gain his attention and
present her "request which comes close to a claim" for good land.[45] Ratner
similarly describes Achsah as subverting the way her father used her as a
"commodity: by setting her own price and demanding valuable land from
her father."[46] Achsah plays into feminine stereotypes and expectations in
a patriarchal society to achieve her aims.[47] McKinlay captures the various
ways Achsah can be read, though she is more skeptical and raises questions about what it means for this woman to be involved in gaining land
through conquest.[48] McKinlay proposes that Achsah is a "moveable pawn
of Israel's myths of empire"; she is troubled by Achsah, who in many ways
mirrors many people's complicity today regarding how land is claimed.[49]
I was inspired by how McKinlay asked questions of Achsah and wanted
to express this diversity of opinion concerning her in the sermon and not
come down too hard on any single interpretation. The notion of memory
helped me to play with how we remember and present Achsah. Achsah is
a complicated figure: she is neither a completely positive nor completely
negative representation of a woman. This nuance, I believe, is essential to
try to capture in a first-person sermon. If done well, a first-person narrative can try to express these tensions.

The key question for the preacher that pulls the sermon together is:
what do these minor stories say about God? I want the congregation to
learn the importance of sitting with an uncomfortable story and placing
it in the broader biblical narrative. These stories do not sit in isolation but
speak into and inform one another. People need to be able to tell uncomfortable stories and to lament, but also to place their stories in the wider
story of God, which ultimately brings hope. As an evangelical preacher,

45. Bal, *Death and Dissymmetry*, 154.

46. Ratner, "Playing Fathers' Games," 150.

47. Ratner, "Playing Fathers' Games," 152.

48. McKinlay, "Meeting Achsah on Achsah's Land."

49. McKinlay, "Meeting Achsah on Achsah's Land," 39.8.

I make Jesus the major narrative beat and the voice I always want people to come and hear. Traditionally, many evangelical preachers can be taught that a sermon is incomplete unless Jesus is mentioned and not just Jesus but specifically his death.[50] It took me a few years of preaching to shake off this impulse. Now, I concentrate on the biblical text I am trying to preach and am not quick to reduce the text to the same message. In the sample sermon, I try to hint at and express the theme of forgetfulness and forgetting and forgotten. I want people to turn to Jesus, who remembers and welcomes all. In order to facilitate this, at the end of this sermon, another person came up and gave people guidelines, creating a space for the church to lament and reflect on who is in danger of being forgotten today.

Listeners

All preachers need to be mindful of their particular context. An evangelical preacher needs to work out how controversial a counter-coherence sermon might be and what they hope people will do with such a message. It is right for listeners to be suspicious of views that run contrary to deeply held evangelical presuppositions.[51] It is also important to recognize that some people listening will resist the Bible and/or an evangelical reading. A counter-coherence approach is not an appropriate strategy to use every week. However, it is a tool that can be used to hear the minor voices in the Scriptures and highlight the minor voices in the church and wider community. It can "reorient preaching toward the other" in a "radical act" of compassion.[52]

If a preacher is listening to the story of a minor character in the Bible, then the next question should be: who would identify with this character's story today? A counter-coherence sermon can affirm people on the margins now by sharing their stories and helping others listen and become aware.[53] This is the power of stories. They can help us to identify with a whole range of people. Arthurs argues that preachers are called to retell stories from the Bible because they can strengthen a community's memory

50. Campbell, *Jesus V. Evangelicals*, 80–81.

51. Andrew Sloane talks about this in greater detail as he explores Wolterstorff's argument on situated rationality in *On Being a Christian in the Academy*, 79–110.

52. McClure, *Other-Wise Preaching*, 7.

53. Claassens, *Mourner, Mother, Midwife*, 10.

and identity by reminding people of the character of God.[54] Stories can also be an apologetic tool to people who think the Bible has nothing worthwhile to say to them. Using first-person pronouns draws listeners in close to the character and their story. Those listeners who feel marginalized might hear God's love for them by hearing a minor voice amplified.

A counter-coherence sermon can help preachers address current topics in society that are not always discussed in the church. Again, taking Achsah as an example, I wanted to explore erasure and how it intersects with memory and forgetfulness. This works on a few levels—Judges 1 was created by scribes drawing and selecting memories and stories that help form and sustain a religious community and nation. These stories help shape the people's sense of identity. In the sermon, I wanted to gently raise questions about how the standard story is told and question what is missing—namely, women and the claim for land. Bevan writes that in war, there is not just the physical damage of buildings destroyed or lives lost but the deliberate destruction of cultural artifacts, like libraries, to erase "memories, history and identity attached to architecture and place—enforced forgetting."[55] According to the official telling of the story, there were people removed in order for this new nation to come to be. That should trouble us a little, shouldn't it?

Memory and forgetfulness work not only on a national level but also on a personal level. In the first-person sermon, I wanted to create Achsah as an older woman reflecting on her life. This is, again, a decision for a preacher to make—not only choosing which character but imagining from what moment of their lives they are telling this story to us. I repeat lines and structure the sermon as a loop, coming in and out of the present and the past, blurring the lines like memory can function. Given that older women can experience erasure in our culture and church, it felt like an added layer worth including.[56] It was essential, therefore, to make sure as I prepared the sermon that I heard stories of people today struggling with memory and erasure because I wanted to give voice to their struggles through the story of Achsah.[57] Part of the good news we hold on to as Christians is that God remembers. We can live "in the memories of God."[58] A preacher needs to

54. Arthurs, *Preaching as Reminding*, story as a tool for stirring memory, 11.

55. Bevan, *Destruction of Memory*, Introduction.

56. Chasin and Kramer, "Ageism and Sexism." See also Scheib, *Challenging Invisibility*.

57. A wonderful theological resource on dementia is Swinton, *Dementia*.

58. Swinton, *Dementia*, chapter 8.

be aware of the variety of experiences in their church and, where possible, encourage people to share, or, with their permission, share their stories in the worship gatherings. Telling minor stories from our context can help those listening to develop a wider awareness of God's concern for the pain in our lives and those around us.[59] Part of the gospel I want to communicate as a preacher is one of inclusion. Older women are a cohort that can be forgotten, but there are great resources giving further practical actions churches can take to welcome and care for older people.[60]

It does not just stop with the people in the church listening to a sermon. The application should extend to asking: who do people in our congregations see, and who do they not see? There is a tendency for congregations to contain similar people with similar stories. One of the roles of the preacher is to bring God's counter-voice to challenge those areas in people's lives that they might be blind to. This question is needed more than ever, with many commentators discussing the echo chambers we live in.[61] Increasingly, we hear and see people just like us and fail to understand people who are different.

Conclusion

First-person narrative sermons are not new for preachers. Still, having started to preach first-person narratives from a minor character's perspective in my church, I have been reminded of just how powerful they can be for those listening. Bal's counter-coherence theory offers a reason why this might be so. People are longing for their stories to be heard and to know they have value in God's story. Yet women's voices are often muted in the Bible. Bal's approach encourages people to take the time and challenge themselves by listening not just to the dominant or obvious narrative beats but also to the minor ones. In doing so, we can amplify and celebrate a range of voices.

59. Claassens, *Mourner, Mother, Midwife*, 15.

60. Scheib, *Challenging Invisibility*.

61. This a sampling, not an extensive selection of articles discussing the dangers of echo chambers: Hosanagar, "Blame the Echo Chamber on Facebook. But Blame Yourself, Too."; Kristof, "Confession of Liberal Intolerance."

Sample Sermon[62]

> *Read Judges 1:9–15*
>
> *Today, we are entering the book of Judges using our imaginations. This sermon might be different from what you are used to hearing. Christine will be telling us this story from Achsah's perspective. This story from Judges 1 invites us to ask: what do we remember, and what can we forget that we shouldn't?*

Where was I . . . do you remember? There're so many children running around the place, so fast, bursting in and out of the house while I sit here. Who are they? Where did they come from? And whose hands are these? So, sun-spotted and . . . old. This can't be me. I remember running around the place so fast, bursting in and out of the tent, throwing up dust everywhere. I grew up in the wilderness, in the time of our wanderings. I'd run and perch on a stony outcrop and watch the blazing red sun sink into the desert. It was magnificent. Hmmm . . . maybe that explains the sun spots on my hands now. Dry skin, dry throat, this I remember . . . and the smell of smoke.

There was a great fire in the distance . . . scrolls burning. Is that right? Yes, there was a city. They called it the City of Books, Kiriath-sepher. They said it contained stories from the beginning of time, stories and knowledge about the world. Imagine being able to record your life and preserve it forever so that the people who came after you could know who you were. We, of course, have scrolls, precious scrolls, locked away in the ark. They come from Yahweh and tell the stories of our people. I love those times when one of those scrolls is unfurled and read out to us—for a moment, it's like I am there, and I can see Moses climbing up the mountain to meet with God, I can see Sarai laughing behind the tent flap. But we don't have a city of books. My father says the stories in that city are wrong, false. So, they burned the scrolls, and just like that, all those stories were erased, just ash blowing across the desert, smoke in my lungs. I know I shouldn't have, but I felt sad when that city burned.

I felt like it was because of me—all those scrolls disappearing because of me. It was my father helping the Israelites to march forward and claim the land and the cities in the land. It was my father who offered me as an incentive. "Whoever attacks Kiriath-sepher and takes it, I will give him my daughter Achsah as a wife."[63] Is that what he said? Yes, I believe so.

---

62. A recording of this sermon can be found at Redwood, "Achsah's Memories."

63. Judg 1:12 (NSRV).

He would give me away. I was the reward. I remember the buzz around the camp. Some of the other girls were jealous. There were lots of daydreams, lots of talk about who were the greatest warriors, the emerging heroes of our generation. We were waiting, wanting to be married. We thought that's when life really started.

I think I was excited, or maybe I was scared. I could be given to any of those men now preparing for battle. I remember the camp emptying out and then nothing until we saw smoke on the horizon. News slowly filtered back. We had won. The city was ours. And Othniel, my cousin, had led the charge. He had taken the city, my name on his lips. They said he was eager to claim his reward. The wedding happened quickly, not a lot of fuss, not like today. We were still at war, after all. It was very simple—I was wrapped up in a veil and given to Othniel. He, in turn, gave me a bracelet, heavy gold, and I wondered if it came from that city, what woman had worn it before me.

It was strange at first, being a wife. I mean, I knew Othniel; we grew up in tents not far from one another, and we might have played when we were small kids, running in and out of the tents, but there was suddenly this man beside me at night, just there, removing my veil, wanting to touch me and be with me. He was quick with compliments, charming, and dreaming of what our lives could be. I started to dream, too. Othniel had just been so focused on marrying me that he hadn't considered much beyond that. All he could see was just more marches to lead, wandering and conquering for his father-in-law. But I wanted something new. I dreamed of water and dust turning to mud beneath my feet. I wanted somewhere I could settle and raise a family. No more wandering. And I believed my father had given Othniel a dud deal. I dreamed of a better gift.

At least, that's how my husband tells the story. He loves telling the story at night when I am wrapped up in his arms. His deep voice rumbles. He says I seduced him, removing my veil, eager for him to touch me and be with me. And then afterward, when he's all smiling and satisfied, I convinced him we should approach my father and ask for land, good land. Sometimes, when he tells the story, it changes slightly, and he says it took many nights of me speaking about it, and he got so tired of my nagging that he gave in. Once, when he told the story to others, he said it was his idea from the beginning. It's a delicate balance communicating with your husband, don't you think?

We tell these stories, and every time we tell, we are remembering, but the memory never feels quite there. It slips and unfurls from me. Do you know what I mean? Some say that Yahweh has a great scroll, the scroll of life, where everything is written down and preserved. What would it say about our early days of marriage? For a moment, it's like I am there, and I can see myself lying next to Othniel, and we are kissing and laughing and talking about how we could approach my father. I can see myself lying next to Othniel, and I am trying to have a serious conversation and convince him I am right, but he doesn't want to talk. He's distracted by my body. I can see myself listening to Othniel and promising I will speak to my father. I am lying in bed, and Othniel is asleep. I am twisting the bracelet he gave me, round and round, coming up with a plan. Maybe all these memories are wrong, false. Don't trust me. Burn them up, erase them, let them be ash blowing across the desert, smoke in lungs.

Where was I . . . do you remember? There're so many children running around the place, so fast, bursting in and out of the house while I sit here. Who are they? Where did they come from? And whose bracelet is this? It looks special, expensive. This can't be me. I remember I used to ride. When I was allowed, which wasn't very often, but I loved it. I love being around animals. We had a few cattle, sheep, and donkeys. We all had to work together to care for them, sustain them in the wilderness. Water is crucial. Gulping it down, splashing it on my face, pouring it out for the animals. I love when the storms come and the waters fall from the heavens, turning the dust into mud, crumbling the rock, bringing out the flowers. It's magnificent.

I remember it rained the night before the memorial service. Our great leader, our commander-in-chief, our deliverer, Joshua, had died. And we gathered to bury him and commit him to Yahweh. The ground was damp, with puddles everywhere. My father was up at the front, transformed, thinner somehow, shoulders stooped. It would be his turn soon to pass. That's what I realized. He wouldn't be here forever. His body would be buried, and he'd be gone. Joshua hadn't just been his leader and commander. He had been his friend. It was just the two of them—out of those first scouts who'd come back and believed we could take this land and make it ours. They had trusted that Yahweh could come through on his promises. And they had stuck to that belief even as we continued living and wandering in the wilderness, even as one by one their friends died, and they'd gather to bury them and commit them to Yahweh.

Finally, it was time. We crossed the Jordan and entered the land they said was made of milk and honey. The cities were falling before us, and Joshua was leading the way. But now he is dead, and I can hear the men whispering among themselves—who will lead us? The trumpets blow, and his name is recorded on the scroll. A few quiet days follow, and then the men polish their swords and resume the fighting. Where they can, they give the land and cities new names—Kiriath Arba, now Hebron, Kiriath-sepher, now Debir. I don't ask my husband what it's like, battle. I don't want to dwell on it. I see the smoke on the horizon and think, that will not be me. I will not be erased; I want to live. I turn away from the cities that have disappeared; I turn away from the dead, including my own mother, and instead, I get on my donkey, and I ride out to see my father.

Othniel and I—we need good land. We deserve it. He has worked tirelessly to help his kin find a place they can call home. No more dust, no more blood-red sunsets, no more smoke in my lungs. It is time to settle. I ride on my donkey to my father, and I think about the best way to approach him. I know he has a lot of affection for me, but like many men, he has his pride, too. So, I ride on my donkey towards him, and I . . . I . . . I slide off the donkey and bow down to him, showing him the respect he deserves. In a small voice, I ask, "Please, Father, grant me this special favor, give me some good land, not just dry land, but land with water, springs of water, bless me." No, that doesn't sound quite right. It happened many years ago. You'll have to forgive me. It unfurls from me. I think perhaps I rode up strong and confident, and I clapped at him. He was startled, wondering what was going on, so I leaped into his momentary confusion, and I asserted myself, "Do me this special favor. You gave me away. Now give me good land. We need water so we can flourish, settle, and have a family. Bless me!" After what you have done, selling me out, bless me. Maybe I didn't clap, maybe I just got off the donkey, and I had a conversation with my father. You get the gist. Burn the details up, erase them, let them be ash blowing across the desert. The point is, we were given land, the good land with the upper and lower springs. It is magnificent.

Where was I . . . do you remember? There're so many children running around the place, so fast, bursting in and out of the house while I sit here. They're my grandchildren. I am part of the tribe of Judah, although can I confess a secret? Technically, my father is a Kenizzite. His people lived in the land long before the twelve tribes came and occupied it, but my father made the decision to join this new thing: the Israelite tribes. I'm not sure why. He didn't like to be reminded of his past. He wanted to erase it. Maybe he saw a better future. If he hadn't joined, maybe I would have been one of the women in the burning cities.

The scribes just want names, minimum detail. The scrolls they write on are cramped with their writing. They keep some sort of record—they remind me: I am Othniel's wife, and we have two adult sons, Hathath and Meonothai. Only two sons made it to adulthood. Some of the others died when they were little or just were never born alive at all. Their names are missing. Daughters? Do I have daughters? Sorry, I can't seem to remember. Surely, I do. Or am I thinking about my sister? Do I have a sister? I had brothers, three, I think, Iru, Elah, and Naam. My father's household was big. I hear their names read out, and it helps me remember. There were times I wasn't sure if I would ever experience the blessing of children.

There was this dreadful period, almost eight years when we were attacked and overtaken by the king of Aram Naharaim. Once more, there was fire—this time, it was my fields, my home burning, ash blowing across the land. Sometimes I wonder if all this erasing is worth it, if we are doomed to keep making the same choices, the same mistakes over and over because we keep forgetting. Our priests say bad things happen because we forget Yahweh. But maybe we got it wrong. Maybe taking the land and saying Yahweh had given it to us is wrong. That city of books burning, wrong. And now it is our turn. My husband says my musings are wrong and confusing. He'd rather be out fighting. He mobilizes the tribes and leads the men once more into battle. They celebrate him in the songs now. He will be remembered as a great deliverer filled with the Spirit of God, one who brought us peace.

Where was I . . . do you remember? There're so many children running around the place, so fast, bursting in and out of the house while I sit here. Yes, I remember. I am trying to give you my story. It's not much, not like my husband's. And there's so much I already have forgotten; time is erasing me. People don't like me as they once did. An old woman nobody has time for. I see all these children, and I want them to know they matter. Maybe what I really want is for them to know that I matter, too. I did the best I could with what I had. Am I looking for redemption? I don't know. I can't sleep well anymore. It's like the smoke returns, heavy in my lungs. When I wake, I see this home, waters bubbling and overflowing, dust turning to mud. I want to believe love overflows here, but what about the ash that blew across that horizon? What about the women in that city? Can there be a world where we give without needing to take? Can there be enough for everyone? Fewer cities and homes burning. Maybe we've been telling the story wrong. Forgetting parts we shouldn't. I don't know. It unfurls from me. Please, don't erase me, God.

Do you ever feel like you are forgotten? That your life is insignificant? It is easy to forget the women and their stories in the Bible, but I believe God does not forget them. I see God when I look at Jesus and see how he interacted with and noticed women. We need to tell these small and big stories to hear God's love and concern for all people. Who are we in danger of forgetting or erasing today? Let's pray and ask God to help us remember.

Discussion Questions

Have you ever focused a sermon on a minor character? What did you learn from the experience?

What voices are missing from your church? How can you amplify them?

Name the strengths and weaknesses of a first-person narrative sermon.

Exercise

Choose a biblical narrative and write a first-person narrative sermon. You might think about the different senses to help you inhabit the character. What do we know, and where are the gaps? What does this character experience of God?

3

How can we hear more than
one voice in a sermon?

THE IMAGE OF PREACHING that comes to mind for most evangelicals is of a solo preacher, generally a man, monologuing from the front of a church to a silent congregation.[1] In that monologue, the preacher seeks to speak about the gospel of Jesus Christ. There is one authoritative voice that dominates. Much is implied in such an approach; in particular, it gives the impression that there is only one voice or meaning in the biblical text. Even though I'm passionate about preaching, I wonder if it's the only way to communicate the gospel. My first pastoral role was primarily with young adults; sometimes, they looked bored as I preached. So, I started experimenting with other ways of communicating. We'd have discussion nights when I would facilitate but then give space for people to engage in smaller groups and wrestle with different questions. Sometimes, instead of a sermon, I would invite people from our community to chat up in the front, and we'd hear part of their stories. I am not the only one doing this. In recent years, there have been attempts in homiletics to suggest alternate models, but evangelicals, on the whole, still tend to deliver monologues. When I was training to be a preacher, I loved taking a class on preaching that stretched us to be creative and considered such questions like how people learn. But these discussions tend to stay in the class, and for many preachers, it doesn't impact their default mode of expository preaching.

---

1. A version of this chapter first appeared in Redwood, "Kaleidoscopic Preaching."

This is strange because not only is our culture learning in multiple ways, but the biblical text itself is multifaceted, and I believe this should shape how we communicate it as well. I will take Judges 5 as an example to show what this might look like in practice.

Multiplicity and the Preacher

As I discussed in chapter 1, evangelical preachers seek to listen and follow the main authorial intention. This means they often function like a narrator leading the congregation through a particular story's main plotline and theological focus. The impression preachers can give by using the monological form and focusing on one idea is that interpretation and truth are singular. Taylor argues that Christians often present truth in such a way because Christians are monotheistic; God and truth become intertwined. Truth, therefore, is "never plural, multiple, and complex but always unified, single and simple."[2] This is the impression you can get when listening to evangelical sermons. Yet this univocal practice has been challenged on a few fronts.

Evangelical preachers occupy a position of power and authority in the church. However, this is not granted automatically to female preachers. They have the further complication of trying to establish their authority! Evangelicals like to emphasize that their authority does not come from themselves but from the Scriptures.[3] But in practice, one preacher often results in one dominant authoritative voice. The temptation can be to conflate the preacher's interpretation with the text itself—a major factor contributing to the monologic nature of evangelical preaching. However, this dominance has suffered somewhat over the last few decades.[4] At times, preachers have abused their positions of power or even given oppressive or manipulative sermons (not even always consciously). This has caused people to be a little bit more jaded when it comes to hearing someone preaching. It has also inspired some preachers to rethink how they preach.

Western culture has become increasingly pluralistic and suspicious of one dominant voice or metanarrative. Local or marginalized narratives tend to be more celebrated because of their particularity.[5] Lose gives the

2. Taylor, *Erring*, 175.
3. Chan, *Preaching*, 160–61.
4. Craddock, *Authority*, 1–20.
5. Lyotard, *Postmodern Condition*, 37–41.

example of the internet as a place where many people are going to form their identity. There, they are encountering "alternating, even opposing narratives instantaneously."[6] This has left some preachers wondering how to preach the Christian metanarrative in such a context. Lose argues for a more participatory model of preaching.[7] Some homileticians have proposed more conversational approaches. For example, McClure writes about creating a metaphorical roundtable. He suggests that as part of their preparation for the sermon, a preacher should gather a group from their congregation and ask them questions about what is happening in their lives and even their responses to the biblical text that will be preached.[8] Rose similarly advocates a shift from the mode of monologue to the mode of conversation.[9] She draws on feminist thought when discussing how people form knowledge, arguing it is a more "connected process" than often imagined.[10] She proposes that preaching be seen as part of a broader conversation: it is a partnership between the preacher and the congregation, which is less about hierarchy and more about mutuality.

Multiplicity and the Text

It is not just our changing cultural context; the biblical text itself suggests multiplicity. The Bible holds a variety of genres. Howard believes that the authors/editors of the Bible were highly innovative, responding to the situations they faced, retelling and reworking older texts for new contexts.[11] This can reassure us that "there is neither one right answer to the question of how to live out the faith nor one superior way to tell the stories of our communities and our God."[12] The Bible has this tension between unity and plurality in terms of its literary forms and theological perspectives.[13] Edwards argues that such tensions challenge evangelical expository preaching, with preachers quick to harmonize.[14] It can be tempting to settle for simple black-and-white

6. Lose, *Preaching at the Crossroads*, 104.

7. Lose, *Preaching at the Crossroads*, 105.

8. McClure, *Roundtable Pulpit*, 49.

9. Rose, *Sharing the Word*.

10. Rose, *Sharing the Word*, 22–30.

11. Howard, *Old Testament for a Complex World*, 9.

12. Howard, *Old Testament for a Complex World*, 56.

13. Allen, "Theology Undergirding Narrative Preaching," 33.

14. Edwards, *Theology of Preaching and Dialectic*, 25.

explanations or one big idea and present it to a congregation. Yet the Bible itself pushes against that. Kalmanofsky writes that the biblical texts invite us to read and not "reach neat conclusions related to ideology or character" but instead "embrace" the complicated nature and multiple readings possible.[15] While as an evangelical, I would want to maintain that the author/editor is trying to communicate through the text, that does not automatically mean an evangelical need to subscribe to only one meaning. There are layers to a text. Many evangelicals would acknowledge the polyvalence of meaning in a biblical text. Ricoeur adds that while there is more than one meaning in a text, this does not mean anything goes because the "text presents a limited field of possible constructions."[16] He calls out the extreme of saying the author completely governs the meaning of the text, and we can completely know it, and the extreme of arguing that the text is completely disconnected from the author.[17] Evangelical preachers can recognize the biblical text's meaning as "multi-faceted yet bounded."[18] A preacher can also recognize gaps, particularly in biblical stories and songs. The author deliberately creates these gaps. These gaps invite and "create opportunity for polyvalent interpretation."[19]

An example of polyvalence in the biblical text is the song recorded in Judges 5. As a preacher, a critical decision needs to be made concerning the limits of the text. Judges 5 can be considered alongside Judges 4. Many scholars see an "intentional theological unity" between the prose and poetic accounts.[20] Block describes the two accounts as "two lenses" that the author/editor gives to describe a single event.[21] So, a preacher must decide whether to preach Judges 4–5 together or select just one of the texts. Either option is valid. I have preached Judges 4–5 as a standalone sermon, and I have also preached them separately, dedicating one week to Judges 4 and the following week to Judges 5.

---

15. Kalmanofsky, *Power of Equivocation*, 8.

16. Ricoeur, *Interpretation Theory*, 79. He also speaks about the surplus of meanings that arise in the use of language, particularly when using metaphors. See Ricoeur, *Interpretation Theory*, 45.

17. Ricoeur, *Interpretation Theory*, 30.

18. Brown, *Scripture as Communication*, 85.

19. Powell, *What Do They Hear?*, 22.

20. Hamlin, *At Risk*, 81; Schneider, *Judges*, 83; Way, *Judges and Ruth*, 49; Block, *Judges, Ruth*, 183.

21. Block, *Judges, Ruth*, 183.

Judges 5, in contrast to the narrative of Judges 4, is a song. Therefore, if a preacher is just looking at Judges 5, the poetic techniques of imagery and structure will need to be given special attention.[22] Songs are concerned primarily with evoking "emotions and attitudes."[23] The vivid imagery and playfulness of language remind preachers that we, too, can experiment with metaphors and that the words we use are important for conveying not just information but emotion.[24] The song tells how the Israelites had a remarkable victory against the Canaanites because of Yahweh.

The startling thing about the song in Judges 5 is there are multiple perspectives offered as we are presented with three female characters: Deborah, Jael, and Sisera's mother. This song is also unusual in its focus on women and their experiences. Bal argues that Judges 5 comes from the female tradition.[25] This proposal is fleshed out in greater detail by one of Bal's close colleagues, Fokkelien van Dijk Hemmes, who co-wrote *On Gendering Texts: Female and Male Voices in the Hebrew Bible*. Bal writes the foreword commending this book. She says that scholarship has not taken the notion of female voices and even female authorship in the Bible seriously.[26] One of the key arguments for the possibility of female authorship is evidence that suggests women would most probably have been involved in these texts' early oral production.[27] Alongside this claim is also the assumption that Judges 5 is older than Judges 4.[28] Bal believes that by the time Judges 5 was included in the final form of the book of Judges, it was redacted to fit into the wider narrative.[29] She suggests that the redactors tried to downplay the song's feminine

---

22. Alter, *Biblical Poetry*.

23. Biddle, *Reading Judges*, 55. Alter also describes the different functions of poetry to prose, commenting that the poem in Judges 5 by using parallelism builds a "powerfully heightened representation of character." See Alter, *Biblical Poetry*, 49. Witvliet addresses this when writing about the Psalms and encourages people to consider how this wide range of emotions can be used in our worship gatherings today. See Witvliet, *Biblical Psalms*, 30–32.

24. Taylor discusses this in his book on the Psalms. His words can also apply to the song in Judges 5. He addresses the important role of the metaphor in poetry and the place of emotion. See Taylor, *Open and Unafraid*, 45–46, 57, 63.

25. Bal, *Death and Dissymmetry*, 211.

26. Bal, "Foreword," ix.

27. Brenner and van Dijk Hemmes, *Gendering Texts*, 19.

28. Bal, *Murder and Difference*, 1.

29. Bal, *Murder and Difference*, 112.

elements, but it managed to survive because of its popularity.[30] Even if people are not convinced by these arguments and Judges 5 was not written by a woman, Van Dijk Hemmes (and presumably Bal) would still argue that the text is presented from a woman's perspective. There are female voices that explore the dangers for women in wartime.[31]

Bal criticizes interpreters for concentrating their attention more on Judges 4. This happens partly because the narrative appears first and partly because it depends on "masculine focalisation" and is, therefore, more comfortable for many readers.[32] It also happens because there often exists a tension between prose and poetry forms, with poetry considered less "precise" and, therefore, less historically true.[33] Most scholars concur, though, that the song is older.[34] Yet, because it is not so much a narrative, many readers favor the story more than the song. Bal wants to focus and tell the story of Judges from the margins, and so for this reason, she attends to Judges 5. Bal argues that the focaliser in Judges 5 is a female. In Judges 5:1, the narrator informs the reader that the song is written by Deborah (Barak's name is also present, but Bal believes it was inserted to soften the feminine voices in the song).[35] The reader then experiences Deborah's account. This is an example of what Bal calls "character focalisation."[36] Bal distinguishes between internal focalization from a particular character's perspective and external focalisation, which is what the narrator chooses to select and "gaze" at.[37]

In Judges 5, multiple perspectives are given as the three women tell snippets of their stories. These perspectives collide with one another. This seems to be part of the author's intention. As we progress through Judges 5, each woman is further from the norm: first, there is an Israelite woman, then a non-Israelite woman who helps Israel, and then a woman who is considered an enemy. What ties these women together is the motif of motherhood. The various women express what it means to be a mother in three different ways. When I read Bal's work, I am reminded how sin (not that

---

30. Bal, *Murder and Difference*, 112.

31. Brenner and van Dijk Hemmes, *Gendering Texts*, 48–58.

32. Bal, *Murder and Difference*, 115–24.

33. Bal, *Murder and Difference*, 76.

34. Scholars who argue that the poem is older include: Wellhausen, *Prolegomena*, 242–45; Vaux, *Early History*, 748; Noth, *History of Israel*, 151.

35. Bal, *Murder and Difference*, 112.

36. Bal and Boheemen, *Narratology*, 105.

37. Bal and Jobling, *Story-Telling*, 91–92.

Bal uses the word "sin") impacts the most vulnerable, leading to terrible acts of violence. In the time of the judges, women tended to be the victims of this violence (as is, unfortunately, still the case today).[38] The temptation can be to downplay the brutal aspects of the song and not acknowledge the horrors.[39] This is perhaps what Bal and other feminists are reacting to. Bal's response is to listen, especially to the women who have suffered. There is a polyvalence of appropriate responses to a text. This response seems to fall "within the parameters of meaning invited or envisioned by the narrative."[40] These female characters are present in the text. They become part of a chorus of voices speaking about the consequences of sin and grace breaking through and redeeming the situation.

Preachers need to consider how this multiplicity can be conveyed through a sermon. Smith proposes rather than a monological hermeneutic, Christians should adopt a creational hermeneutic. This is a hermeneutic that celebrates a diversity of interpretations "not as the original sin but rather as primordially good."[41] This looks like creating "room for a plurality of God's creatures to speak, sing, and dance in a multivalent chorus of tongues."[42] The preacher can allow the text's various focalizations to move them to "consider the lives and viewpoints of those whom we normally consider as the Other."[43] A preacher may take many strategies, but the strategy I'd like to propose I have named *kaleidoscopic*. A *kaleidoscopic approach* seeks to embody multiple voices and perspectives in a single sermon.

This draws on a recent shift in homiletics. Preachers have begun to be influenced by fiction and film and reflect on the implications for preaching. Brown encourages preachers to think like a filmmaker and create a sequence of scenes, thinking about each scene as having a "distinct function, or effect for the listener" and also working together to tell the overall story.[44] According to Brown, one of the goals of the sermon is not simply to pass on information about God but to "help us see and feel the consequences of the wrongs we do, and imagine new possibilities."[45] Fiction writers know

38. Gerhardt, *Cross and Gendercide*, 91.
39. Trible, *Texts of Terror*, 86.
40. Powell, *What Do They Hear?*, 5.
41. Smith, *Fall of Interpretation*, 59.
42. Smith, *Fall of Interpretation* 184.
43. Park, "World of the Judges," 240.
44. Brown, "Designing the Sermon's Form," 161.
45. Brown, "Designing the Sermon's Form," 164.

that it is not just about creating scenes but that writers need to choose what perspective they will tell the story from. That choice will affect a reader's experience of the story. Mills explains that a reader's "sympathy is usually reserved for those characters whose viewing positions we are allowed to occupy, and withheld from those we are not."[46] Yet this knowledge is rarely considered when it comes to preachers communicating stories from the Bible. This is particularly concerning because one of the consequences can be a lack of women's voices and perspectives in evangelical preaching.

In a *kaleidoscopic approach*, an evangelical preacher could deliberately choose to amplify multiple voices in a sermon. One of the functions of stories and songs is creating empathy—as we hear the biblical story, people identify with one or more of the characters.[47] Yet Powell says this can happen at an unconscious level, potentially shutting down the "possibility of experiencing the story from an alternative point-of-view."[48] Chenoweth uses the word "refocalisation" to describe how writers can tell a well-known traditional story from a different perspective and suggests there is a role for biblical fiction to do the same.[49] A reader/preacher's social location can be a factor in influencing where our empathy will go.[50] One of the ways a preacher can counter this bias is to read the biblical story and ask themselves who they identify with in the narrative and then read a second time and try to occupy a different role. Chenoweth calls this method "casting the scriptures."[51] Such an approach opens a preacher up to notice the polyvalence in the text. He suggests you can choose the unexpected perspective and allow that perspective to shape your sermon or retell the story from different perspectives and invite multiple responses from the congregation. I build on his method by proposing preachers can retell a biblical story using multiple first-person perspectives.

For example, in the sample sermon, I experimented with embodying all three female characters in Judges 5: Deborah, Jael, and Sisera's mother. I also wrote a fourth voice to help transition between the three women. I asked another person to assist by being the narrator/theologian to help listeners navigate the different stories. A preacher can start in the same

46. Mills, *Writing in Action*, 107.

47. Powell, *What Do They Hear?*, 29.

48. Powell, *What Do They Hear?*, 30.

49. Chenoweth, "Biblical Fiction," 288.

50. Chenoweth, "Biblical Fiction," 31.

51. Chenoweth, "Biblical Fiction," 60–61.

way any first-person narrative sermon begins by stepping into the text's gaps and imagining. I imagined details about Deborah's life. For example, I say in the sermon:

> My father used to travel up and down the highways, and then when the Canaanites came into power, law and order broke down, bandits and robbers took to those same highways, and my father was killed. I ran and ran until I found this tree where I could collapse and shriek and howl.

I draw from Judges 5:6–7, which speaks about life at that time, and then personalize it by weaving it into Deborah's story. Similarly, I take the references to rape in Judges 5:30 and incorporate that experience into Jael's story:

> A soldier came into my tent. He reached out and grabbed me, pinned me down. When I tried to fight back, he struck my head. At his feet, I sank, I fell, and there I lay. I don't have to tell you the rest, do I, you know what happens to women? I'm sure you have heard how the soldiers brag: this tent is mine, this girl is mine.

It was very confronting, to talk not only about rape but to come to a point where I speak of murdering Sisera. I had to really dig into trying to understand what could motivate Jael.

Using a first-person perspective structure is a choice that limits a preacher in many ways. If you are bound to one perspective, you are trying to speak only from that perspective, which means, for instance, if I'm telling the story of Judges 5 from Deborah's perspective, I can't then speak about Jesus. These limitations are also the strength of first-person perspectives—listening to first-person narratives can often feel more intimate as you listen to someone who "doesn't know the full story, or gets it wrong, or isn't telling the truth."[52] There's something very human and relatable that people listening can connect with. Expanding first-person narratives to include more than one voice suddenly expands our view of God. It allows us to wrestle with the ethical dilemmas often present in the biblical narrative/song(s), like how one person's justice might not feel like justice for another person.

Giving voice to three different characters requires preachers to reflect on embodiment. There has been discussion in the homiletical field on the importance of embodiment, particularly how preachers use their

---

52. Grenville, *Writing Book*, 61.

own voices and facial and physical expressions to convey the story.[53] This is even more of a consideration when trying to capture multiple characters when giving a sermon. In my example sermon for Judges 5, I set up three stools. For Deborah, I was most like my usual preaching self. I moved my arms and alternated between the stool and standing. Then, for Jael, I tried to drop my voice slightly. I did not look at the congregation as much, and I crossed my arms and kept myself closed as much as possible. Even when I stood, I did not move from that spot. In contrast, for Sisera's mother, I relaxed again, spoke in a slightly higher pitch, crossed my legs, opened up my hand gestures, and paced up and down, occupying more space. There is a conversation in homiletics about how much preaching should be "natural" and how much of it is "performance."[54] This has been further complicated for women because what has historically been perceived to be natural is how men occupy the pulpit space. Many women have turned to the theater to help them explore how to use space.[55] Part of the role of preaching, says Ward, is to develop this "sense of the other," assisting listeners to engage with those who are different from them, perhaps on the margins, and ultimately to help people engage and encounter the presence of God in this space.[56] By being intentional in the areas we occupy, we can help people encounter God and others who are different from us.[57]

Multiplicity and Listeners

When a preacher gives space for more than one voice, it can prepare our listeners for this reality in our church and in society. This, Park suggests, is particularly relevant in our currently fractured society. She says Judges 5 pushes us to occupy different roles and experiences than our own.[58] Lane writes that one of the functions of good application is "reversal," to help listeners find themselves identifying with the unexpected characters and seeing a glimpse of themselves in them.[59] By inhabiting these different

---

53. McKenzie, "*Actio Divina* and *Homo Performans*," 64.

54. McCullough, *Her Preaching Body*, ch. 5.

55. McCullough, *Her Preaching Body*, ch. 5.

56. Ward, "Performance Turns."

57. This resonates with Chopp's work when she says feminist theologians can help people to reimagine. See Chopp, *Power to Speak*, 20.

58. Park, "World of the Judges," 240.

59. Lane, "Application and Persuasion," 67–68.

characters, I became convicted in a way I had not been until practicing the sermon, that Sisera's mother was the woman I most identified with. I say as her:

> I promised myself my son would want for nothing. He'd have the best. He'd be the best. And he was, right from the beginning, he was so quick, quick on his feet, quick with his words, adored by all. Every privilege was his. We'd play with tiny chariots, lining them up in a row, moving them across the floor, play with tiny soldiers marching in a line, pretend to be in sword fights.

I am a privileged woman. Most of my church is privileged, we want the best for our children, and we can ignore (or we are blind) to our complicity in wider systems that cause other children to experience injustice.[60] Application in evangelical preaching tends to focus on actions and the will.[61] A sermon like this can counter that. I encouraged the congregation towards empathy and to wonder whether we are more like Deborah and Jael, who long for justice and change, or more like Sisera's mother, who is comfortable with the status quo.

I also intentionally drew in a range of modern female voices to help connect this ancient biblical text to our contemporary context. I amplified three different female poets in the sermon. The first woman is a Kurdish poet, Benjan Matur, who experienced persecution and torture in Turkey for being Kurdish. She says:

> That's how I started writing poetry. In my head. To bring back to life an existence they were trying to obliterate. My poems are about the reconstruction of a shattered being.[62]

I wanted to amplify a voice that seems so removed from my life in Australia, to challenge my listeners to hear marginal voices in our world today. I drew on one of Matur's poems, "Every Woman Knows Her Own Tree," which describes a bird landing on a tree crying out in pain.[63] Matur's words helped me get into Deborah's character and discover her voice. The image of a tree reminded me of the palm tree where Deborah sat. The second female poet I amplified is the pop singer Halsey and her poem, "A Story Like Mine," which

---

60. Thelle argues that all the mothers in Judges 5 are complicit in different ways justifying "wartime rape and violence." See Thelle, "Matrices of Motherhood," 450.

61. Capill, *Heart Is the Target*, 24–26.

62. Vulliamy, "Voices above the Chaos."

63. Matur, "Every Woman Knows."

she read aloud at the 2018 Women's March.[64] Her voice speaks more into our immediate context and the recent discussions women have had where they long for an end to sexual, gendered violence. The third female poet I drew on was Ghada Alatrash, who grieves over the loss of life in the recent Syrian conflict. The song in Judges 5 is primarily a victory song, but there is also a hint of lament and some compassion, even for Sisera's mother, that I wanted to capture. There is loss on both sides in any conflict. To help my listeners identify with Sisera's mother, I bounced off these words from Alatrash's poem "Um [mother of] Muhannad," which speaks about this mother performing the ritual of having breakfast with her son, always trusting another day is coming.[65] Then, her son is killed in an explosion. The application for the listeners is to empathize with people unlike them and continue to long for change and God's justice/mercy to come. It is important to be aware that if a preacher addresses something deeply personal, it is appropriate to warn people that this sermon could trigger emotions. This can be done before the service through a weekly email or even before the sermon starts. If a preacher is preaching sensitive stories, they also need to provide a space for people who might need to debrief or pray afterward.

Lastly, as we reflect on multiplicity in the text, we must also acknowledge a multiplicity of listeners. It's a tricky balance to navigate since most preachers will develop a particular style of preaching, which can be hard to expand. Part of my journey, which this book reflects, was about learning to find and embrace my voice. Yet I recognize my style leans towards stories, imagination, intuition, and drama. This differs from many evangelical preachers I have heard, who tend to be more ideas-based. Listeners can experience frustration when they don't connect with a preacher's style. A listener who by nature is more deductive and linear can hear a sermon like this and wonder: what was the point?[66] To counter this, a preacher needs to try different sermon structures as much as possible. Jeter and Allen recommend preachers to be "multilingual in homiletical" forms.[67] I would also encourage there to be a team of preachers with different styles who will connect with different people.

64. Halsey, "Story Like Mine."

65. Alatrash, "When a Mother."

66. Jeter Jr. and Allen, *One Gospel, Many Ears*, 11.

67. Jeter Jr. and Allen, *One Gospel, Many Ears*, 13.

Conclusion

There is a discussion in hermeneutics around polyvalence in both interpretation and the biblical text. There is also a conversation happening in
homiletics on how to communicate in a pluralistic culture, which is often
suspicious of those who claim authority. I want to encourage preachers to be
more willing to play and try different approaches to preaching. Evangelicals
have the opportunity to not just amplify one marginal voice but include a
diversity of voices in a sermon. I have suggested one direction, a kaleidoscopic strategy that builds on the first-person narrative form and extends
it to include other voices. No longer will the dominant image of evangelical
preaching be a man monologuing to a quiet congregation but of a range of
voices and points of view that invite imagination and participation in speaking and living out the gospel that lies at the heart of evangelical identity.

Sample Sermon[68]

Today's words are not easy.
And yet we trust God is here.
These are words formed in the context of war.
Something, thankfully, mostly unfamiliar to us.
But not for everyone in our world.
This is an ancient poem.
One of the oldest songs in the whole Bible.
And what do we hear?
We hear the voices of women speaking about war.
A rare thing to hear.
Today, we will hear three voices.
They come from Judges 5.
There is imagination involved this morning,
And other contemporary female poets have shaped this telling.
As we enter Judges 5,
Some hope for things to change, and others want things to stay the same.
Each story begins simply with:
I am a mother.

68. A recording of this sermon can be found at Redwood, "Hear Their Voices."

Deborah

I am a mother to my people. The Canaanites came, crushed us, when I was just a child. We lived in a small village, trying to grow enough food to eat. All the families would work together, sharing what we had. My cousins and nieces and nephews all lived nearby. My father was a trader, and what we couldn't grow, he'd go down into the valley and trade. There was singing, lots of singing, as we'd gather outside in the evenings after a hard day's work, and my father and my mother would sing and tell stories about our people. My favorite stories were the ones that featured Miriam, the woman who praised God with a tambourine when they walked free out of Egypt. She sang: "Yahweh is my strength and my might, and he has become my salvation."[69]

Those were good days before everything became a lot harder. My mother searching through empty cupboards, trying to cook a meal for us to eat. When she found old bread, that was a win. My father used to travel up and down the highways, and then when the Canaanites came into power, law and order broke down, bandits and robbers took to those same highways, and my father was killed. I ran and ran until I found this tree where I could collapse and shriek and howl.

Under that tree, in the middle of my grief, that's when the God of Sinai spoke, calling me to be a prophet, a mother to Israel. I started to sit under that palm tree between Ramah and Bethel in the hill country. I'd sit and pray for my people, pray for God to act. I'd stare up at the green fronds, watching them move in the breeze day in and day out. And pray, God, do something. I know you can.

Others started to sit with me. They wanted me to pray for them; they wanted to hear from the God of Sinai. And so, I'd pray, and sometimes I'd share a word with them. And those words were recognized to be true. More people came, and I started to settle disputes. I became a judge. I realized how wayward my people are, like children, as I heard the complaints and petty arguments. Some days, I got so frustrated. No wonder the Almighty One had not rescued us! But other days, my heart would break as I'd sit with someone crying because their loved one had been killed on the roads, or they were being evicted from their house and land because they couldn't pay the taxes the Canaanites imposed. It was hard enough, at the best of times, trying to grow a crop that would feed everyone, but the taxes kept

---

69. Exod 15:2 (NRSV).

getting higher and higher, squeezing us all dry. Village life ceased. If something didn't change, we'd soon cease.

A fire burned inside me as I heard my people's stories, each story fueling that fire, so it grew and grew. I became angry at the Canaanites who enjoyed such luxury while we struggled, and I became convicted that God wanted us to act. So, I spoke. I wanted my words to burn those who heard them, spark my people into action. At night I dreamed of palm trees lighting up the darkness like torches, the flames leaping from tree to tree. We couldn't be scared any longer. That's what I said, "Don't be scared, let's act, God is with us, rise up! It's time to sing again." I started to dream of Yahweh marching towards us, coming from the land of Edom: the earth-shaking, the heavens pouring down water, the mountains quaking before Yahweh. God is on the move.

These sons and daughters of God had been entrusted to me. And so, like any mother, I wanted to protect them. That's what a good mother does, right? Protects her children, keeps them safe? Brings new life. I could see this people needed someone to lead them and so I acted. I called Barak to me. I said, "Barak, you are going to be the commander of our army. We are going to have an army. Remember the songs of old, the voices of the singers at the watering places. They recite the victories of Yahweh. Wake up, arise Barak! Take captive your captives, son of Abinoam."

Barak and I rode along those highways, calling on the tribes to come out. Some came from Ephraim and Benjamin and from Zebulun and Naphtali. The princes of Issachar were with me. I was so excited to see this spark of hope growing. The tribes gathered at Mount Tabor, getting ready for what was to come. But not everyone turned up. In the districts of Reuben, there was much searching of heart but no action. Gilead stayed beyond the Jordan. And Dan, why did he linger by the ships? Asher remained on the coast and stayed in his coves. Not all the brothers came, but I reassured the people. I said it was okay. I am the mother of Israel, and I know God is with us. You are not risking your lives in vain. This fire cannot be quenched.

So Sisera, commander for King Jabin, came with his iron chariots. He faced us, and then we fought. We fought by the waters of Megiddo, and the heavens, the stars they fought with us, the river Kishon fought against Sisera, that age-old river, sweeping the chariots away. March on, my soul, be strong! Then there was the thunder of horses' hooves galloping away, and we cheered as the Canaanites ran, defeated. God showed once more that he can be a warrior to those who cannot otherwise defend themselves. He came and fought for the villages, for the peasants, and now we have a chance to live.

> *If you were to write a poem,*
> *What would it say?*
> *Would you focus on personal struggles,*
> *The struggles of a nation or go even wider?*
> *What are your prayers full of?*
> *You, your family, or do they go further than that?*
> *Deborah's prayers went far beyond herself.*
> *She longed for change for her people.*
> *Benjan Matur is a Kurdish poet.*
> *She grew up persecuted in her country for being Kurdish.*
> *When she was twenty years old, she was arrested and jailed for twelve months.*
> *Because she was Kurdish and a law student, she was viewed with suspicion.*
> *She started forming poems while sitting in the darkness of a prison.*
> *She longs to see change in her country.*
> *Who will hear her voice?*
> *Can God be here—in these complex struggles?*

Jael

I am a mother to all those daughters out there who have suffered. What else do you need to know about me? What do you want to know? Maybe not much. Maybe you don't want to get too close. Maybe you are scared of me. I get it. Most people are. They give me a wide berth. Even before I did what I did. I mean, I am not really one of you. I am not an Israelite. I am a Kenite. A Kenite far from home. My mother named me the wild one, like a wild goat. I was born with lots of dark hair, born strong, and a bit rebellious. I hated being told what to do all the time; my father told me to be still, to be silent. But my mother, when he wasn't looking, she raised me to be strong. Then war came to our land, and I realized I wasn't strong at all. A soldier came into my tent. He reached out and grabbed me, pinned me down. When I tried to fight back, he struck my head. At his feet, I sank, I fell, and there I lay. I don't have to tell you the rest, do I, you know what happens to women? I'm sure you have heard how the soldiers brag: "This tent is mine, this girl is mine." I lost my sisters in war. The soldiers came and took many away.

I was left behind; I don't know why. My parents quickly married me off to a man named Heber. Heber wanted to be safe, so he left our people and took me with him. I never saw my mother again. He made deals with whoever was in power. He promised to be an ally to the Canaanites. My husband collaborated with Sisera, telling him whatever he needed to know: any hint of rebellion was quickly squashed. It disgusted me the way my husband groveled to that man, the way I was meant to grovel to him.

I heard about this prophet, a woman prophet calling Israel to fight. I dismissed it at first. I mean, what can a few villagers do? But the Israelites are a strange people. They believe in a strange God, a God of justice. I'm not even sure if I believe in the gods. If they are there, I don't think they care about us much. My husband ordered me to stay in my tent, stay safe. And then he left to scout out more information, find out what was happening so he could tell Sisera all about it. I waited in that tent for a long time. I waited until I could hear a battle taking place in the distance. The walls of my tent quivered and shook, just like they did when I was a young girl.

Just like when I was a young girl, I heard footsteps thundering towards me. I peered out, and there was a bloody man running right at me, a sword by his side, and I wanted to disappear, but he saw me, so I pretended I am strong. I stepped out and realized it was Sisera running towards me. I politely greeted him while my heart started to shake: does this mean the Canaanites have lost? Can it be true? I informed him my husband was not here. But he didn't care. He was agitated, glancing this way and that, and the sword moved with him. I stammered . . . "Would you like to come in?" I did not expect he would say yes. A man does not enter a woman's tent. But he did. He came in because, after all, he is not just a man. He is a soldier. And a soldier can do whatever they want, take whatever they want.

I decided I would try and be like a mother to him. Maybe if he was reminded of his own mother, I would be okay, and he wouldn't try anything else on me. He asked for water, and so I brought him some. I said, "Do you want milk with that as well?" I expected him to say no; it's children who drink milk, but he said yes. So, I opened a skin of milk and gave him the drink, and he gulped it down. It splashed everywhere, running down his beard and neck. I handed him a blanket, and he looked at me like he was waiting for more. I ignored his look and instead tucked him in, nice and tight, and as I watched him fall asleep, this crazy idea suddenly came into my head.

This is it. This is my opportunity. I can get back at him. For all he and his army have done, done to my sisters, my friends, me. The violations they took, the way we were treated as if we were nothing, a girl or two for each man, the spoils of war. Whatever they want us to be, we are: sex slaves, mothers. Both. Look how he has strolled so confidently into my space, ordering me around like he owns it.

My hand reached for the tent peg, my right hand for the workman's hammer. This is for all the girls who have been wronged by him and those like him. I wanted him to feel what they felt. I struck Sisera with all the force I had. I struck him on the forehead, I penetrated him, crushed his head, shattered and pierced his temple. His eyes opened in shock, and then he fell, rolled off the bed, dead. I am a mother to all those girls. And we say: "No more. You will not harm any more of us." You tell me, you be my judge—was I wrong to put a stop to such a man? Who else will stand up and put a stop to the violence so many of us have endured?

> *If you were to write a poem*
> *What would it say?*
> *There are some stories that feel too uncomfortable to say out loud*
> *at church.*
> *Some poems we don't want to share with anyone.*
> *Halsey, a pop singer, wrote a poem detailing her experience with*
> *sexual assault and rape.*
> *It's confronting; you can look it up afterward,*
> *It's called "A Story Like Mine."*
> *She finishes:*
> *"There is work to be done*
> *There are songs to be sung.*
> *Lord knows there's a war to be won."*[70]
> *Do such words belong in a sacred space?*
> *Jael is called blessed.*
> *Can God be here in this messy struggle?*

Sisera's mother

I am a mother to my son. My only beloved son. The moment I first held him in my arms I was overwhelmed with love, and if I am to be honest, relief. I

70. Halsey, "Story Like Mine."

had borne my husband a son. I had fulfilled my duty. And I was rewarded with new gowns and a beautiful necklace for my efforts. I named him Sisera. I promised myself my son would want for nothing. He'd have the best. He'd be the best. And he was, right from the beginning, he was so quick, quick on his feet, quick with his words, adored by all. Every privilege was his. We'd play with tiny chariots, lining them up in a row, moving them across the floor, playing with tiny soldiers marching in a line, pretend to be in sword fights. He was always good at getting the other kids to do what he wanted them to do. A real leader, charismatic and charming.

I loved to spoil him with whatever his heart desired. Dressing him in the latest fashions, buying him a horse so he could learn to ride. Then he left so he could learn how to be a real warrior. The day he first left home, I remember I got up early, got the slaves to light the candles and pack his meal: bread, cheese and yogurt, dried fruit, and water. I made sure it was arranged just the way he liked. Whenever he came back home this became our little ritual. I would wake up early and prepare the table for us to eat together.

My son grew into a strong and powerful man, rising up the ranks to quickly become the commander of the Canaanite army. And he started to spoil me with whatever my heart desired. Bringing expensive cloth and jewels, all for me. I love it; I love him. Whenever he left, he'd grab my two hands, kiss them one by one, and say, pray for me. And I did. I'd get out the little statues, and I prayed. His work is dangerous. So sometimes, I even paced up and down the halls. I peered through the windows as I waited for news. Waiting is the worst.

A boy ran one day to my home, bringing news, not the news I wanted to hear, but still news. The Israelites had risen up. They were trying to overthrow our glorious king, King Jabin. I relaxed. They are weak; my boy would put it to a halt in no time. Establish law and order once more. I started to imagine what spoil he'd bring back. Spoil is one of the best parts of war. The men get their reward, a slut or two for each man, and I can get more colorful garments, beautiful embroidery for my walls. I peered once more through the lattice, muttering to myself, "Why is his chariot so long in coming? Why is the clatter of his chariot delayed?" My ladies answered me. I had forgotten they were there. They mumbled platitudes, reassuring me he would be fine. I am a mother, and I want my son home with me.

If you were to write a poem
What would it say?
Sometimes, we don't long for change.
We like the way things are like Sisera's mother.
This song in Judges 5 stretches our empathy.
We need our empathy stretched.
We need to hear different voices,
Learn to put yourself in someone else's shoes.
Then justice might come.
Jesus could sit with all different types of people,
Hear them, and then challenge them.
Change is coming. Justice is coming, Mercy is coming.
Are you ready?
What is your prayer this morning?
We are going to have some space now,
For you to write to Jesus
As a way of responding.
Giving voice to your struggles,
Giving voice to others and their struggles.
If you are brave, you can even leave them on the communion table
for others to read.
May all who love you, God, be like the sun
When it rises in its strength.

Discussion Questions

Have you ever considered what the monologue format implies about the Scriptures and God? What are the strengths and weaknesses of the monologue approach?

Do you believe preachers have authority? How do you exercise such authority? What are ways we can safeguard the pulpit from abuse?

Are there other places in the Bible you can think of where a multiplicity of voices are present?

Exercise

Choose a biblical narrative where there is more than character. Write or tell the story from one of the character's perspectives and then tell the same story, but this time tell it from the other character's perspective. Alternatively, you could even try and partner with someone else—you take one character, the other person takes the other character, and then come back and share what you have written. Reflect on this exercise—what stood out when you heard two perspectives? Where was the overlap? Where was the difference? What did you learn about God hearing two different perspectives?

4

How does the country I am preaching in shape my sermons?

I HAVE SPENT A lot of time reflecting on what it means to be a female preacher but very little time reflecting on what it means to be an Australian preacher.[1] I just assumed it was not that different from being an American or an English preacher. When I started engaging with the feminist scholar Esther Fuchs, I encountered postcolonial theology. While Fuchs has not written a commentary on the book of Judges, she has written multiple times about the story of Jephthah's daughter. The first was in a 1989 article titled "Marginalization, Ambiguity, Silencing." This was then adapted and included in her 2000 book *Sexual Politics in the Biblical Narrative: Reading the Hebrew Bible as a Woman*. More recently, she has revisited the story in a chapter of her 2016 book *Feminist Theory and the Bible: Interrogating the Sources*. This time, she is reading it from a postcolonial and a feminist perspective.

This opened up a new dimension for me to consider.

Postcolonialism is a literary theory that critiques/questions Western epistemology. Postcolonial biblical hermeneutics is a growing field that emerged in the 1990s and seeks to counter dominant Western narratives.[2] Scholars R. S. Sugirtharajah, Fernando Segovia, and Keith Whitelam are

---

1. An earlier version of this chapter appeared in Redwood, "Preaching and Postcolonialism."

2. Segovia, "Mapping the Postcolonial Optic," 46.

critical figures in postcolonial biblical studies.[3] These scholars consider how land, race, and power are addressed in the Bible and applied in contemporary and historical contexts.[4] Postcolonial scholars are trying to fight against the continuing effects of colonialism as perpetuated by the West.[5] Its aim is liberation from such "dominant structures."[6] Two groundbreaking works in this field are Edward Said's *Orientalism* in 1978 and Gayatri Chakravorty Spivak's essay "Can the Subaltern Speak?" in 1988. These works reveal the (often unconscious) presuppositions that Western interpreters bring to the text. The Bible has been used as a way of justifying the colonialism that has taken place.[7] There are also postcolonial feminists. These scholars argue that there is an "intricate relationship between colonialism and patriarchy and seek to hold these tensions together in their analysis."[8] A key concern for postcolonial feminism is how women are portrayed in the biblical text and how that portrayal links to power and "colonial domination."[9] While researching Fuchs, I spent a lot of time delving into her postcolonial feminist reading of Judges 11–12. The sample sermon below shows how my Australian identity was brought into a conversation with this particular biblical text. As preachers, we have the opportunity to speak, often prophetically, into our national conversations.

Postcolonialism and the Text

Judges 11 tells the story of Jephthah. He is noted for his power, yet his birth origins are unconventional and lead him to be driven out of his father's house by his brothers. When Ammon attacks Jephthah's old homeland, the elders of Gilead take the initiative and come to him. They want him to fight for them and are willing to establish him as a leader. He agrees and, once

---

3. Classic works include: Segovia and Tolbert, *Reading from This Place*; Sugirtharajah, *Voices from the Margin*; Kwok, *Discovering the Bible in the Non-Biblical World*; Whitelam, *Invention of Ancient Israel*. More recent works include Butler, "Joshua-Judges and Postcolonial Criticism"; Moore and Segovia, *Postcolonial Biblical Criticism*; Perdue et al., *Israel and Empire*; Gossai, ed., *Postcolonial Commentary*.

4. Dube, *Postcolonial Feminist Interpretation of the Bible*, 16–17.

5. Kim, "Postcolonial Criticism."

6. Sugirtharajah, *Postcolonial Reconfigurations*, 15.

7. Kim, "Postcolonial Criticism."

8. Kwok, *Postcolonial Imagination and Feminist Theology*, 80–81.

9. Kwok, *Postcolonial Imagination and Feminist Theology*, 81.

established as their leader, embarks on a diplomatic mission to Ammon. The narrative slows at this point with a lengthy monologue covering Israel's history, land, and theology.[10] The negotiations fail, but Jephthah sounds confident in God. As the two groups prepare for battle, it is not surprising that confidence is confirmed with the Spirit descending on Jephthah. But then Jephthah makes a vow to God, promising to sacrifice whatever comes out of his house for victory over the Ammonites. The Israelites defeat the Ammonites, and Jephthah returns home to celebrate. There is no mention this time of the land experiencing peace (as in Judges 3:11, 3:30, 5:31, 8:28). Instead, the mood abruptly shifts when Jephthah's daughter comes out of his house, and Jephthah remembers his vow to God. His daughter asks for time to prepare herself before allowing her father to sacrifice her life.

Fuchs argues that postcolonial hermeneutics has tended to focus on the role of the foreigner in the biblical text and not the role and development of the nation of Israel. Fuchs seeks to use a postcolonial framework to explore the intersection of the nation with feminist concerns. Fuchs is interested in how masculinity and femininity are wrapped up in Israel's national identity, which is also in the process of construction in the book of Judges. She reflects on other feminist interpretations, applauding them for bringing the critical theme of Judges 11, which she believes is "male violence against women," to the forefront of people's minds.[11] The most troubling aspect of this story for many is the sacrifice of the daughter and the silence surrounding her death. There seems to be no condemnation by God, the characters, or the narrator, and no attempt by anyone to stop the sacrifice. However, in Fuchs's most recent work, she critiques feminist scholars for failing to ground this private violence in the broader "context of warfare and public violence."[12]

For Fuchs, the book of Judges is concerned with forming, articulating, and preserving a new national identity as the twelve tribes of Israel begin to come together as one nation.[13] In Judges 11, that national project is threatened by the Ammonites. To maintain the new nation of Israel, men need to be warriors. Fuchs defines the masculinity portrayed in Judges 11 as strong

---

10. Webb, *Book of Judges*, 316.

11. Fuchs, *Feminist Theory*, 79.

12. Fuchs, *Feminist Theory*, 79. This critique is also made by McClintock, an author Fuchs cites in her chapter on Judges 11. See McClintock, *Imperial Leather*, 355–56.

13. Fuchs, *Feminist Theory*, 40.

and violent.[14] Nationalism and patriarchy join forces to legitimize and authorize "masculine hegemony."[15] The Ammonite threat ends when Jephthah leads the men into battle and defeats the Ammonites, thus preserving the nation. There is also an internal threat to Israel's nation-building project. In Judges 12, Ephraim seems to question Jephthah's right to be a national leader. In response, Jephthah quickly battles and defeats Ephraim and his cohorts.[16] But this conflict shows the ruptures among the tribes. It subtly points to the need for a monarchy to be established for Israel to function as a stable nation.[17] National identity is interwoven with gender identity.

Fuchs interprets the femininity in Judges 11–12 in contrast to this militarized masculinity. Femininity is associated with domesticity and victimization. This has terrible consequences for women who frequently experience violence, not just from outsiders but also from their own community. The surprise in the narrative is that the national hero, Jephthah, ends up killing the woman in his care rather than protecting her. Fuchs makes sense of this in a few ways. First, she argues that the external threat creates a military system that secures the nation but damages Israelite women. Second, this story teaches that other nations' influence on Israel can lead them into idolatry and morally bankrupt practices and cause even their national hero, Jephthah, to stumble and sacrifice his daughter.[18] Fuchs concludes that the national narrative promotes masculine violence as necessary to secure the nation even though a high cost is required.[19]

One of the strengths of Fuchs's work is the way she exposes how masculinity and femininity are interwoven with nationalism and how damaging these particular visions can be. Evangelicals will have differing views on whether masculinity is presented in this way in the book of Judges. Most scholars just accept that men needed to be warriors in this period. Esler writes that because Israel was such a small nation, "warfare was always going to be a major element in its continued existence."[20] Wright agrees that in the book of Judges, we see that if a man desires to

14. Fuchs, *Feminist Theory*, 80.

15. Fuchs, *Feminist Theory*, 80.

16. Fuchs, *Feminist Theory*, 83.

17. Fuchs, *Feminist Theory*, 83.

18. Fuchs, *Feminist Theory*, 81.

19. Fuchs, *Feminist Theory*, 88.

20. Esler, *Sex, Wives, and Warriors*, 141.

rule, he needs to be a military leader.[21] Yet Wright goes on to say that the author/editors of Judges "cast dark shadows on any attempt by a military hero to acclaim too much honor," like Jephthah.[22] For Wright, the editors of the book of Judges want to challenge the ideology that equates "the warring king with the warring god."[23]

Fuchs suggests that when women are depicted and encouraged to be submissive, this can have damaging consequences. Greves, a Pentecostal scholar, suggests the daughter, far from being simply submissive, critiques her father. Greves points to verse 36, where the daughter exposes her father's "self-centredness" by emphasizing "your enemies" rather than saying "Israel's enemies."[24] Then Greves, similar to Fuchs, suggests that the daughter represents "Yahwistic faithfulness and family—two values inherent to Jewish identity."[25] Yet this connects with Fuchs's objection—these traits lead to the daughter's demise. Sometimes evangelicals do not seem particularly troubled by what happens to the girl. Block condemns Jephthah's actions against his daughter and names them as a form of abuse, but a few sentences later celebrates the daughter as a "victim of faithfulness."[26] This is the very thing Fuchs is critiquing: that the daughter has become a model for women to follow. Block continues by saying, "and in her fate she represents all the courageous daughters of abusive fathers."[27] Block celebrates her faithfulness as courageous![28] She is faithful and does not protest, and it leads to her death. Block wants to distinguish different forms of patriarchy, saying Jephthah's form was wrong but that softer forms are acceptable. I am not convinced. One of the reasons this is so damaging is that it can make domestic abuse easier. This is a live issue in our contemporary context. McCann similarly addresses this issue, arguing that this text reminds us that not all suffering is "virtuous and redemptive."[29] The girl's death is

21. Wright, "Military Valor and Kingship," 36.

22. Wright, "Military Valor and Kingship," 48.

23. Wright, "Military Valor and Kingship," 52.

24. Greves, "Daughter of Courage," 164.

25. Greves, "Daughter of Courage," 166.

26. Block, *Judges, Ruth*, 378.

27. Block, *Judges, Ruth*, 378.

28. This line of interpretation can also be found in other works like Baker, which celebrates the daughter for putting her own community's interests above her own. See Baker, "Power That Cannot Be Named," 77.

29. McCann, *Judges*, 88.

not like Christ's death because it has been caused by "idolatry."[30] I push
back against this reading in my sermon:

> *I want to say, to the women out there especially, it's not always a*
> *good thing to be the good girl. Look at Jephthah's daughter—not*
> *as someone to admire or copy but as a warning. She was a good*
> *girl, and her father lit her up, set her body on fire, and watched her*
> *burn. Even faithfulness is not always a good thing—Jephthah and his*
> *daughter were faithful but to something so deeply wrong.*

Fuchs is interested in how the nation-building efforts harm women,
particularly Israelite women, so she doesn't address how the surrounding nations are portrayed, nor does she discuss how Jephthah's story in
Judges 11:14–27 contributes to the nation-building project and could be
problematic. But through her, I encountered other postcolonial writers
who raised these concerns. Kim, for instance, writes how the surrounding
nations function in the book of Judges as villain figures oppressing Israel;
this threat brings the Israelite tribes together, helping to form the nation of
Israel into a "coherent community."[31] To be foreign is to be wrong.

The natural inclination of evangelical preachers is to side with Israel.
Evans briefly acknowledges that there are often "different interpretations
of history" but then proceeds to affirm that Jephthah is like a "scholar
historian" accurately recounting the true story of the land.[32] Evans continues that the theological application of this story is that Yahweh decides
which nation will win and get the land.[33] Having read Judges 11 now from
a postcolonial perspective, this theological application raises troubling
implications that I believe evangelicals need to grapple with. Warrior addresses the conquest narratives and argues that "the Canaanites should
be at the center of Christian theological reflection and political action.
They are the last remaining ignored voice in the text, except perhaps for
the land itself."[34] Hamlin is sensitive to how this text could be read, saying
there is "the danger of smugness or even arrogance" in Jephthah's argument that "military victory implies divine approval."[35] This can lead to
those who are more powerful taking whatever they want and claiming

30. McCann, *Judges*, 88.

31. Kim, "Politics of Othering," 174.

32. Evans, *Judges and Ruth*, 129.

33. Evans, *Judges and Ruth*, 131.

34. Warrior, "Canaanites, Cowboys, and Indians," 264.

35. Hamlin, *At Risk*, 116.

God sanctions it. Evangelicals must pay critical attention to how this story has been applied, particularly when used in modern nations' formation, and critique damaging applications.

Prior, who is interested in exploring how colonizers have used the biblical traditions of land and conquest, says that the book of Judges, unlike the book of Joshua, hints at some of the complications and even at times hints of "Israelite bad conscience at dispossessing others."[36] In Judges 11, we see Jephthah going to great lengths to justify the Israelite occupation of the land. McCann, an evangelical scholar, writes that the book of Judges has been used to "legitimate violence" against other people groups and nations "rather than to pursue God's creational purposes."[37] McCann justifies Israel's actions to remove the Canaanites, explaining that God is not against a particular ethnic group but opposes a "way of life based on injustice."[38] Hamlin acknowledges that it seems like Israel has "special privilege" on the surface because they claim to worship the God and Judge of all the nations, and at the same time, they have a special relationship with that God.[39] But Hamlin argues that Israel was meant to model something different. Then, along traditional evangelical lines, he presents the surrounding nations as the primary oppressors who lead Israel astray and cause them to adopt similar values.[40]

Another typical evangelical response is from Burge, who argues that all land belongs to God and that "land and righteousness are linked."[41] The Canaanites lost their land because of their sinfulness, and then, in the book of Judges, the reader learns that Israel faces the same possibility.[42] When people sin, their security in the land is threatened by oppressing nations. God sends these nations. This is something I have preached in the past. Burge's book promotes justice and peace for Palestinians now, and I was persuaded when I first read it. Yet when I opened it again, I noticed how the conquest was permitted in the past because the "Canaanites promoted a religion utterly inimical to God's law," in contrast to Christians and Muslims who live in

36. Prior, *Bible and Colonialism*, 229.

37. McCann, *Judges*, 17.

38. McCann, *Judges*, 19.

39. Hamlin, *At Risk*, 115.

40. Hamlin, *At Risk*, 111.

41. Burge, *Whose Land?*, 86.

42. Wright, *Mission of God's People*, 457–61.

Palestine and Israel today.[43] Evangelicals argue that the conquest commanded by Yahweh was a one-time occurrence, specific in that particular time, and to apply such commands now would be deeply inappropriate.[44] The question remains: is it ever acceptable to invade and conquer if people do not follow Yahweh? After engaging with a postcolonial reading, the evangelical approach seems too simple and neat.

Yet, as an evangelical, I also have questions about how a postcolonial reading works with this ancient text. The first complication in this story is trying to determine who is the colonizer. Is the daughter a daughter of a colonizer or the colonized? The daughter seems to represent someone pure: her virginity is emphasized as a good thing. This purity further justifies Israel's right to the land. Yet, the fact that she is a virgin hints that she is young. Judges 10:7–8 tells us that the Ammonites and Philistines conquered Gilead and oppressed the Israelites for eighteen years. This shifts my understanding of the daughter to someone who has experienced colonization rather than being a colonizer. Suddenly, Jephthah becomes a liberator. Hamlin takes this perspective, naming Ammon as a "powerful force" who uses "political means (colonialism)" like so many powerful nations today to gain control of the land.[45]

The second complicating factor is whether colonization is even the appropriate framework to understand the original conquest of the land. Colonization is described as an "imperial process."[46] Yet Israel was never really an empire and is not an empire in the book of Judges. Neither is the Ammonite nation. They are a collection of tribes competing with other tribes for land. These tribes are not strange and distant others but part of Israel's family. In Genesis 19, there is the disturbing story of Lot (Abraham's nephew) having sex with his daughters. The youngest daughter gives birth to a son from whom the Ammonites are said to be descended. In Deuteronomy 2:19–20, as the tribes of Israel are coming into the promised land, they are commanded not to dispossess the Ammonites, for their land has been given to them by Yahweh. The Ammonites and the Amorites were never destroyed: they continued to function as tribes/nations alongside Israel until empires swallowed up them and Israel. The conflict described in the books of Joshua and Judges seems more tribal and localized. In other

43. Burge, *Whose Land?*, 84.
44. Burge, *Whose Land?*, 84.
45. Hamlin, *At Risk*, 123.
46. Ashcroft et al., *Empire Writes Back*.

books in the Old Testament, Israel must grapple with the reality of actual empires conquering and exiling them from the land.[47] Wright proposes that the whole Old Testament canon sits within a postcolonial framework. After the exile, Israel had to form a new national identity and reimagine what it means to be a people.[48] Telling ancient war stories in exile helped encourage national identity and service.[49] The book of Judges, Wright goes on to say, sits in this wider narrative and serves as a bridge between glorious national war stories and the disintegration of the state.[50] The stories in the book of Judges are part of this wider wrestling of what it means to be a people when imperial powers have come and destroyed so much.

Even the framework of nationalism could be potentially misleading. While Judges 11 may be described as a national narrative, we should be careful not to import modern ideas of the nation into this ancient text. Hamley is an evangelical scholar who would agree with Fuchs; she argues that one of the major themes of the book of Judges is national identity, with the authors/editors exploring the "liminal state" of the people to define themselves and to define the Other.[51] Hamley would also agree with Schwartz, who reminds us that in ancient times, the boundaries between different people groups tended to be determined by the "worship of different deities."[52] Sometimes, this can still be true when we see religious violence erupting. Such a conflict is usually a battle over which God will reign over a nation.

Postcolonialism is a complicated idea to understand and apply in our contemporary context, let alone an ancient context. As discussed in chapter 1, evangelicals shaped by their presuppositions want to understand the ancient text as much as possible. Therefore, they can be cautious about using frameworks like postcolonialism. I think some of that caution is appropriate, especially regarding a story like Judges 11–12, which seems to be less about empires swallowing other smaller identities and nations and more about tribes fighting and tribes beginning to form into small nations. However, postcolonialism raises some critical questions—it encourages readers to look at the surrounding nations and think about how they are

47. Perdue et al., *Israel and Empire*.

48. Wright, *War, Memory, and National Identity*, 7.

49. Wright, *War, Memory, and National Identity*, 78.

50. Wright, *War, Memory, and National Identity*, 169–70.

51. Hamley, *God of Justice and Mercy*, 5.

52. Schwartz, *Curse of Cain*, 121.

portrayed. It gives these nations space to become three dimensional and not simply perceived as the "enemy." Postcolonialism also cares about how these ancient narratives have been applied in destructive ways in lands and nations today. It forces evangelicals to confront, acknowledge, and work through how the Bible has been complicit in justifying wars and conquests of other people's land. Lastly, in light of Fuchs's reading, we must recognize that the bringing together of nation and gender has been under-explored by evangelical scholars, perhaps because they tend to be male and Western.[53] They can be blind to how religion can be used and abused in forming national identities and women's identities.

Evangelical preachers preach christologically. This is important to remember when considering Old Testament texts on nation and land. Jesus challenges ideas around the nation and does not see God's kingdom as a "stable territory."[54] It is important for Christians, says Sider, to constantly resist the "temptation of idolatrous nationalism."[55] Woodley and Sanders argue that Jesus' whole life was about resisting "the goals of the empire."[56] They note that one of the weaknesses of postcolonial theology is that it tends to remain theoretical rather than engaging in praxis; it can be hard for people outside of the academy to engage with it.[57] This is something that evangelical preaching could seek to change. Heaney suggests that, in practice, this means learning to read with those "who experience disempowerment," including characters in the Bible.[58] I have come to recognize the value and need to hold together both resistant readings of the biblical text and more reparative readings. Paynter argues that both should be "held together in creative dialogue."[59] The stories we tell about our nation matter. We can name concerns about how the Bible can intersect with nationalism and gender in perilous ways. We can use our imagination to interact with these ancient stories and let them speak into our context.

---

53. An Indian evangelical female scholar writes about how she began to become aware of how much Western theology was influencing her mind and failing to take into account her culture. See Lalitha, "Postcolonial Feminism," 75.

54. Nausner, "Homeland as Borderland," 129.

55. Sider, *Scandal of Evangelical Politics*, 225.

56. Woodley and Sanders, "Was Jesus an Evangelical?"

57. Lozano and Roth, "Praxis in Postcolonial Criticism," 185–87.

58. Heaney, "Evangelical Postcolonialisms," 41.

59. Paynter, *Telling Terror in Judges 19*, conclusion.

Postcolonialism and the Preacher

Fuchs voices some of my initial thoughts when I first read this story, particularly around the daughter. The daughter is once again a minor character. As an evangelical female preacher, reading Fuchs has challenged me to ask hard questions about how much patriarchal ideology I have absorbed. Am I just like the daughter in the story mirroring her father? Suddenly, words that are so familiar have become uncomfortable. I hear evangelical worship songs, prayers, and sermons constantly talking about God using masculine language. God is our Father; Jesus is the Son. In many sermons, I now notice I used the masculine pronoun "he" or "himself" to describe God.[60] It did not trouble me until I started reading feminist works, and now I wonder how these words still subtly seem to imply that being male is normative and better. As a female egalitarian preacher, I am endorsing this position. Neuger is another scholar who writes, "there is much at stake when our primary images and metaphors equate God with a white, male ruler because it contributes to a culture in which white male rulership is seen, at the least, as normative and, at the worst, as divinely sanctioned."[61] I am trying to embrace more neutral and inclusive language in my preaching, particularly when referencing God, but I find it hard. It feels clunky, particularly in oral communication. Sanders is one scholar who has spent time analyzing a range of sermons written by women and noting key themes that seem to be common—the use of inclusive language is one of those themes. She writes that women are more likely to use inclusive language when speaking about people and God.[62]

The impact of colonialism on my preaching is another area I had given little thought to. Travis has written a powerful book on postcolonialism and its implications for preaching. She argues that preachers must "search their own sermons, culture, experience, and relationships for colonising discourse."[63] In the sample sermon, I look at the daughter as a citizen of her nation. Then, I intersect her story with my own as a privileged woman in my nation. I weave Jephthah's daughter and her story with my Australian story. The idea is to combine these two stories by incorporating common words and images. In a sense, I am like the daughter in Judges 11: I am an

60. I have deliberately left this in throughout this book as a reminder that this is where I started when I first began this project.

61. Neuger, "Image and Imagination," 163.

62. Sanders, "Woman as Preacher," 213.

63. Travis, *Decolonizing Preaching*, 144.

Australian whose family not long ago immigrated to this country. I started preparing the sermon by talking to my grandparents and parents. I wanted to connect the national story to my personal story. This is one way we can bring the abstract into the particular. I am also starting where I know.

> Once, my family were migrants. One side of my family fled Ireland and tried to start again in Australia. They were poor. My grandfather would once a week get into the communal bath on his street. The kids would take turns as the water grew colder. My family worked hard, worked on the great national projects of the day—driving trucks for the army, typing for the Snowy Mountain scheme, working in the airport, the oil companies, providing admin to the high schools, playing rugby league on the side, scraping together enough to have a house in the suburbs, to see their children get more than they ever did.

The Australian story, like the Israelite story, is complicated. The stories we tell about the past, just like the stories Jephthah tells in Judges 11 and Judges 11 itself, are active. As Whitelam points out, stories from the past are used "to provide the legitimation and justification of the present."[64] Whitelam argues stories in the Bible bring land and nation together so that Israel is perceived to be superior, more civilized, and the "ultimate in political evolution" compared to the old Canaanite tribes, which are silenced.[65] Western nations have continued this practice. Such nations view themselves, like Israel, as "the pinnacle of civilisation."[66]

This is how the story of Australia is often subtly framed. Pascoe argues that British colonizers believed they were superior, and it was their duty to spread "their version of civilisation and the word of God to heathens."[67] This belief made them ignore their encounters with other people. Aboriginal people in Australia have traditionally been described as simple "primitive hunter-gatherers," yet Pascoe contends that the picture is "much more complicated."[68] At the time of the invasion, Aboriginal civilization was complex, with many "social, agricultural and philosophical achievements" that we

---

64. Whitelam, *Invention of Ancient Israel*, 21.

65. Whitelam, *Invention of Ancient Israel*, 56.

66. Whitelam, *Invention of Ancient Israel*, 56.

67. Pascoe, *Dark Emu*, 3.

68. Pascoe, *Dark Emu*, 3. Ironically Pascoe's work has recently been critiqued for simplifying and de-emphasizing the importance of hunter-gathers. See Sutton and Walshe, *Farmers or Hunter-Gatherers?*

can learn from today.[69] It is only recently that this other story is starting to be told: a story of dispossession, failing to recognize the Indigenous peoples of the land, and, in many instances, eradicating them.[70] In a sense, Australians are living in a postcolonial setting.[71] Australia was a British Empire colony working towards its own national sovereignty and a colonizer.[72] Unlike many other postcolonial nations, it did not achieve sovereignty through violence but remained closely linked with Britain. Postcolonial scholars are not just interested in a state achieving sovereignty, but they also investigate colonialism's lingering "cultural legacy" on that state.[73]

Yet this reality has not always entered into or been named in my church experience. It is as if many evangelical churches are blind to the racism and injustice that has been and continues to be perpetuated in our lands. Budden writes that the "churches in Australia have internalised the values of an invading society" so we do not see the injustice.[74] This damages everyone, but decolonization can transform a whole society by bringing liberation and healing.[75] Smith, writing as an evangelical who is also interacting with postcolonialism, says that one of the ways evangelicals can respond to this context is to "explore the social memories of others and seek to uncover the conscious social 'forgetting' of others' stories within our own cultural narratives."[76] The churches I have been involved in have begun to wrestle with this issue in the last five years. It can look like marking significant days for Aboriginal Christians, introducing acknowledgment of country in our church services, or having Aboriginal Christian leaders come and speak. Brooke Prentis has played an important role in the Australian context, calling the church to respond.[77] Prentis preaches that we must "walk together

---

69. Pascoe, *Dark Emu*, 227.

70. Saunders argues that Australia cannot be a postcolonial nation until the legacy of colonialism has been resolved and Aboriginal sovereignty has been legally recognized. See Saunders, "Post-Colonial Australia."

71. Boer, *Last Stop*, 4.

72. There is an even more complicated story outside the scope of this book, including Australia's relationship with colonies or protectorates like PNG and East Timor and our role in fighting wars on behalf of more powerful empires.

73. Saunders, "Post-Colonial Australia," 1.

74. Budden, *Following Jesus*, 7.

75. Curtice, *Native*, 105.

76. Smith, "Embracing the Other," 198.

77. Prentis worked through Common Grace, where she sought to educate the Australian church. See "Common Grace."

and commit to being led by Aboriginal and Torres Strait Islander Christian leaders to pursue friendship and reconciliation in our lifetime."[78] Part of that work, I believe, is reading stories by Indigenous Australian authors.[79] While I have begun this engagement with Aboriginal leaders and think- ers, I am still learning how it can significantly shift my preaching. In the sample sermon, I try to address this directly. I speak about my Australian story, which contains privilege and pressure to be silent and look away. I am conscious that I have power that not every woman does. I also do not want to presume to speak other people's stories, but I want to wrestle with my complicity. I want to explore how it damages me when these other stories are downplayed and how it damages others.

Fuchs contends that the daughter in Judges 11 is both an insider and an outsider in her nation. I am also, as a female, both an insider and outsider in my nation. I am, furthermore, an insider and outsider in the evangelical church. I am an insider because I have participated for a long time in evan- gelical churches, studied at an evangelical college, and was ordained as an evangelical pastor. Yet, I have felt like an outsider as a woman leading in a church. I have tried to be a good girl in order to be accepted. This becomes the motif I use throughout the sample sermon. Lauve-Moon, researching female preachers working in the Cooperative Baptist Fellowship, observes women, because they experience forms of marginalization in the church, are more likely to identify with other forms of marginalization.[80] They are more likely to take risks and speak out on a wide range of social justice issues even though they know their marginal position.[81] Interacting with feminist and postcolonial theology has changed me, and I am unsure if the wider evangelical church would accept that change. I speak about the pressure to be silent in my sermon. There, I am talking about the nation. I could just as easily be talking about the evangelical church.

78. Prentis, "Walking Together."

79. Recent fiction works which shaped my sermon include Winch, *Yield*; Lugash- enko, *Too Much Lip*.

80. Lauve-Moon, "Preacher Woman," 2.

81. Lauve-Moon, "Preacher Woman," 3.

Postcolonialism and Listeners

Part of the role of a preacher is to be a listener. Van Harn describes "preachers as pioneer listeners on behalf of the community of faith."[82] This means listening deeply to both the biblical texts and their cultural context. Local preachers need to know their congregation, their listeners. Tisdale describes preachers as needing to become "ethnographers," paying attention to the "subcultural signs and symbols of the congregations they serve."[83] Lane concurs, saying that when preachers take the time to know and listen to their congregation and then apply the text in a way that speaks to them, it strengthens the "pastoral relationship."[84] It might be easy for an evangelical preacher (especially if they are privileged) to miss the effects of colonialism on their community. Travis has begun to think about how a postcolonial perspective will shape a preacher's thinking regarding their listeners. She says they will need to "acknowledge the variance of colonial/imperial experience and memory among worshippers."[85] Most of my listeners share my privilege. In my sample sermon, I want them to be uncomfortable and challenged. Du Mez discusses the American context in her book *Jesus and John Wayne*; she focuses on how religion and nationalism are coming together in dangerous ways in our time.[86] Though Australia is not America, there are certainly parallels that I draw on in my sermon. There is an opportunity for preachers to challenge the national narratives. This can be fraught with preachers quick to take a certain political stance, aligning themselves with party politics, or simply failing to ground their words in the gospel of Jesus.[87]

> Yet lately I have been hearing new voices, perhaps these are not new for you, but these voices say: my home is not safe and stable, I was ripped away from my mother, stolen. I couldn't relax and play like you. My brother was thrown into prison for petty theft. I have lost my language, the stories of my people. My future is not full of promise. I hear voices protesting on the streets of Sydney for their young people locked away, deaths in custody, for the way the system brutalizes, ignores them.

82. Van Harn, *Preacher, Can You Hear Us Listening?*, 15.
83. Tisdale, *Local Theology and Folk Art*, 60.
84. Lane, "Application and Persuasion," 66.
85. Travis, *Decolonizing Preaching*, ch. 2.
86. Du Mez, *Jesus and John Wayne*.
87. Markham and Hardin, eds., *Prophetic Preaching*.

I should not assume that all share my privilege. There may be people in our church with Indigenous heritage and people on the margins of our nation, such as recent migrants and refugees. I try to address all three possibilities in my sample sermon.

Fuchs explores the stories that Israel told in its quest for a national identity. Such an exploration is important for contemporary listeners as well. We need to consider the stories that Australians tell themselves. We also need to be aware that biblical stories have been employed in modern nation-building. Boyd describes how Western countries (in his context, he is primarily referring to the United States) have used the stories of Israel to justify invading other lands and seeking to establish "one nation under God."[88] Australians have a complicated relationship and history with our land. Lake traces how biblical stories were used to justify British expansion into Australia in the past.[89] The Bible shaped the colonial farmers' ideas about what farming the land should look like.[90] It was assumed that people needed to bring order into the wilderness, transforming the bush into productive land for the capitalist system. Yet, the Bible was also used by a minority of Christians to speak out against the violent aspects of colonialism. Some argued that the Indigenous people of Australia were also made in the image of God.[91]

More recently, Adam argues that, while there are a few instances of God reallocating land in the biblical narratives (particularly in the book of Joshua), the overarching theme is that all land and peoples belong to God and that theft of land is wrong.[92] We see this concern in the debate Jephthah has with the Ammonites. He stresses how Israel did not go beyond the limits God had set. Naden uses similar language when explaining the Indigenous theological view that God "apportioned his creation to his created humanity," and the land now called Australia was given to the Indigenous peoples.[93] The nations, including Israel, are held accountable by God. For the nation of Israel to stay in the land of Canaan, the people needed to be committed to the covenant, emphasizing justice and love for

---

88. Boyd, *Myth of a Christian Nation*, 148.

89. Lake, *Bible in Australia*, 86.

90. Lake, *Bible in Australia*, 88.

91. Lake, *Bible in Australia*, 99.

92. Adam, "Australia—Whose Land?"

93. Naden, "Aboriginal Land."

the alien and poor.[94] If Israel failed to keep the covenant, they, too, would be "vomited" from the land.[95] The Old Testament narratives show the realities of nations and land with all their complications and sin. Naden suggests that the church must be "made aware of the marginalization and social disadvantage" that Indigenous people face.[96] However, this seems easy for us to forget. For example, young Aboriginal people are still dying in custody.[97] This is part of an old story. Harris wrote about the same issue in 1990, lamenting that "the community is not more horrified."[98] This is what I am seeking to do in this sample sermon. A sermon doing this type of work is only the beginning; ultimately, relationships are needed. Narratives give nuance to these discussions and lead to some fresh thinking for Australians about our connection to the land. It matters how we live in this place, and I believe there is work that needs to be done to help churches to repent and begin/continue the work of reconciliation.

Conclusion

I have been reflecting on what it means to be a preacher in a postcolonial context like Australia. Postcolonial theories often stress the importance of thinking about the country we are preaching in. The Bible has been preached in destructive ways to promote colonial thought, which Australian preachers should be conscious of and seek to change. Australian preachers must consider whose voices and stories are missing and how this may potentially damage others and our witness to Jesus. By engaging with postcolonial readings, I have discovered new questions to ask the biblical text. I found things I had previously missed. This is the value of dialoguing with people who have different perspectives. It can enrich your preaching and impact your congregation.

94. Burge, *Whose Land?*, 110–11.

95. Lev 18:25 (NRSV)

96. Naden, "Aboriginal Land."

97. Allam et al., "474 Deaths Inside." This is again a complicated issue. There are some Aboriginal leaders, like Jacinta Price, who argue the real problem is not Black incarceration but the issue of domestic violence in Aboriginal communities. See Price, "Not the Answer."

98. Harris, *One Blood*, 672.

Sample Sermon[99]

Jephthah's daughter was a girl with many privileges. She was an Israelite. She had a family that loved her, provided for her. She lived in a home that was stable. Where there was more than enough food to eat whenever she wanted, where there was freedom to laugh with her friends, lie under a tree, and gaze at the sky and clouds above. She had the opportunity to learn, learn how to dance and sing, learn the stories of her people, their language, their history. And the future before her was full of promise—of one day having the opportunity to fall in love, to raise her own children and see them flourish.

Her family has lived on this land for a long time and worked on this land for generations. It didn't come easy to them. Once, her family were migrants. Poor migrants. They had to strap their babies to their chests and flee the land they were living in because it was too dangerous. Crossing borders, giving birth without assistance, they fought to secure a place that was safe, that they could call home. God gave them this land. And her family worked hard, worked on the great national projects of the day—serving as soldiers, scraping together enough to have a house, to see their children get more than they ever did. The lucky country, this certainly is a country worth defending. The celebrations get bigger every year, marking the wars they have fought and won; the stories get bigger of soldiers caring for their mates. This is her home, her people, her nation. What wouldn't she do for her country?

Her homeland is threatened, she is told. By others who keep trying to cross the borders, dispute the borders, by the hordes invading. She is vaguely aware of this news, but she never paid it much attention, sheltered as she is. She knows the Ammonites are the bad guys. They tell lies. She knows not to trust anything that comes out of their mouths. They say this land is theirs. These are a people who want what she has and will do whatever they can to take it from her——come in the night, break down doors, steal anything that is of worth. There is only one way you can respond to such a threat.

You defend yourself, right? You go to war. And her father is going to lead the charge. What a man. She is so proud of him with his crisp uniform, his strength, and conviction. She is proud to be his daughter. She listens as he talks to the men in their village: You need to be aggressive, face them

99. A recording of this sermon can be found at Redwood, "Resisting Bad Theology."

head-on. Crush them before they crush you. The Ammonites have been winning for too long. Now it is time to take back what is ours, be men. She cheers from the sidelines. She prays before going to sleep each night: God save us. She watches as all the men empty out of their homes onto the streets and follow her father into battle. She had never felt more proud to be an Israelite than when she sees all her men leave for war. This time, she pays more attention to the news. She hears how the Ammonite King refuses to recognize Israel's claim to the land. Hears her father is preparing for battle. Hears of their great victory. The Ammonites defeated.

Then, her nation calls on her.

Her father calls on her.

She comes out of the house with a tambourine

Wanting to share in this victory.

She comes out of her house singing and dancing.

For her father and his army which have destroyed twenty towns, driving their enemies away.

Her father tears his clothes when he sees her.

Her father calls to her, tears in his eyes:

Take one for the team.

For the good of the nation

He says, "I have made a vow to God.

I asked God for victory and I promised God that

Whoever meets me out of my house

I will sacrifice as a burnt offering.

And you have stepped out.

Would you be willing to lay down your life?

Your country needs you.

God needs you."

The answer is obvious,

She is, after all, a good girl

Always wanting to please,

Of course, yes.

Nobody says to this daughter—no. This is a bad idea. God wouldn't want you to do this. Nobody tries to stop it and say this is not good for the nation or for you. Resist. You need to resist bad theology. They say God wants this. God wants more violence. The war wasn't enough, now violence needs to spill into people's homes. Look out. Beware of the danger of interweaving God with the nation. But, of course, there is no resistance. Jephthah's daughter is a good girl. She has been raised to be obedient to her father, to the men in her life, to be obedient to God. That is what it means to be a woman. And what it means to be a man—is to be a strong warrior leading your family, like her father does. If he says it's okay, it must be okay. She's a good girl. A virgin. She doesn't mess around with any boys. She is waiting until she is married. She wants to be a good mother. Yes, she is privileged, but it doesn't save her. She does all the right things, and it doesn't save her. She is a good citizen, someone to remember. Her tale will be told in the generations to come—this is the story of our people. God was with us, giving us a great victory, and we gave our best to God. We gave our daughter to the flames. And she went willingly. What a sacrifice. Some say, "This story is horrible, but at least Jephthah was faithful to his vow, at least his daughter was faithful. What a model for the next generation of men and women."

My family has lived on this land for a long time and worked on this land for generations. It didn't come easy to them. Once, my family were migrants. One side of my family fled Ireland and tried to start again in Australia. They were poor. My grandfather would once a week get into the communal bath on his street. The kids would take turns as the water grew colder. My family worked hard, worked on the great national projects of the day—driving trucks for the army, typing for the Snowy Mountains scheme, working in the airport, the oil companies, providing admin to the high schools, playing rugby league on the side, scraping together enough to have a house in the suburbs, to see their children get more than they ever did. A generation or so later and, their descendants live in bigger and better houses, no longer eating skinned rabbits. Their children go to uni, get good jobs. The celebrations get bigger every year, marking the wars Australia has fought as a nation. The stories get bigger of soldiers caring for their mates, the worth of our homes grow. This is my family, my people, the lucky country. What wouldn't I do for my nation?

I am an Australian woman with much privilege. I have a family that loves me. I grew up in a home that was stable. Where there was more than enough food to eat whenever I wanted, where there was freedom to play and laugh with my friends, lie under a tree and gaze at the sky and clouds above. I had the opportunity to learn, read as many books as I wanted, enroll in multiple degrees. I learned the stories of my people, their language, their history. And the future before me is full of promise.

But I wonder if there is something I must give in return for all of this. Some say our way of life is threatened. By others who come by boat wanting to cross our borders and get in, by the hordes invading. We must protect and keep them out. Let our government do what it needs to do. Be a good girl. Stay quiet and show your support. Some say our way of life is threatened from within by people who say: hang on, this is our homeland. You were not the first. This land wasn't empty when you came. God didn't promise this land to you. I missed this story in my schooling: I heard about Captain Cook and his great discovery, I heard about how migrants have contributed to this country, but I didn't hear much about the indigenous people of this land. I didn't hear anything from the church, from all the sermons and Bible studies I grew up with. I never thought about my skin color. I took it for granted, just like I took it for granted that white men teach in the church. That's just normal. And if you asked me, I would have said: racism doesn't exist here in this place anymore, not really.

Yet lately, I have been hearing new voices. Perhaps these are not new for you, but these voices say: my home is not safe and stable. I was ripped away from my mother, stolen. I couldn't relax and play like you. My brother was thrown into prison for petty theft. I have lost my language, the stories of my people. My future is not full of promise. I hear voices protesting on the streets of Sydney for their young people locked away, deaths in custody, for the way the system brutalizes, ignores them. They say: you came, and broke us, massacred us, stole anything that was of worth, you did not recognize us in your laws, you made us work for nothing but some rations, you reduced us to nothing. You brought your guns and fired them at us. Not just in the past but now. Injustice is still happening. You have sinned. I want to defend myself. Say it wasn't me. My family had no power. Came long after all that. They worked hard. I want to say, "I am not racist. I am a woman, what power do I have anyway?" There is this anger bursting forth in our land, this grief, and I can hear:

For the good of the nation

People say:

Just ignore the past.

Don't admit any complicity.

Don't admit the way you have benefited from this system.

Isn't my education something I have worked hard for? Sacrificed for?

The land this church is built on—we paid for it. We took nothing away.

Some Christians say, "This has nothing to do with Jesus.

Don't acknowledge your privilege

For the good of the nation.

For the good of the wider church.

Be like Jephthah's daughter.

Be a good girl.

Don't stir up trouble.

Don't ask who is excluded—whose voices you don't hear in the church, in the nation.

Be obedient, and you will be celebrated."

But I am not listening anymore. Instead, I want to say, to the women out there especially, it's not always a good thing to be the good girl. Look at Jephthah's daughter—not as someone to admire or copy but as a warning. She was a good girl, and her father lit her up, set her body on fire, and watched her burn. Even faithfulness is not always a good thing—Jephthah and his daughter were faithful but to something so deeply wrong. Sometimes, we need to resist. We need to resist bad theology. And there is bad theology out there. When it damages people, we are getting something wrong. But too often, we are silent, nobody names it, and then we hear things have been covered up, scandals break out, actually those famous Christian leaders we looked up to were sexually harassing women or worse. We need to resist and name bad theology. We need to resist when theology gets wrapped up in nationalism. It happens a lot; be on guard. Du Mez has written a detailed book looking at recent American history, and she says what we see, particularly among white evangelicals, is:

"An embrace of militant masculinity, an ideology that enshrines patriarchal authority and condones the callous display of power, at home and abroad."[100]

100. Du Mez, *Jesus and John Wayne*, 3.

Nationalism and, patriarchy and theology coming together, just like in Jephthah's day. Now, Australia is not America or ancient Israel. But this pattern of a certain type of nationalism becoming wrapped up with God and certain fixed roles around gender is here in this country. I look back and see how strongly the message to be a good girl and please people became deeply engrained in me. Sometimes, we need to be troublemakers—in the church and in our nation. There are plenty of people who will tell you (both women and men)—not to use your voice, just do what you are told, maintain what is, what has always been. But the truth is:

In the name of Christ, nations have conquered lands,

Christianity came into this land mixed up with colonization.

In the name of Christ, wars have been declared.

In the name of Christ, we are told to take one for the team.

Maintain the status quo.

But we forget who Christ is.

Maybe you already know this, and you are way ahead of me,

But let me remind you once more:

Jesus Christ is and was a troublemaker.

He didn't come to establish the nation of Israel,

He wasn't the national leader they longed for.

He spoke and challenged those in power.

He spoke to the people who were labeled sinners, trouble-makers,

And those with power killed him.

Be our sacrifice for the good of the nation.

Take one for the team, Jesus.

So, we can maintain the status quo. The way things have always been.

But his resurrection disrupts.

Jesus' voice cannot be silenced.

And he says, "It's time to resist,

Both women and men,

A new way, a new kingdom, is coming,

The kingdom of God,

Those who have been on the outside are now on the inside.

I hear the Holy Spirit calling

For the sake of this nation, for the sake of the church

Listen. Listen to the marginal voices that make you uncomfortable.

Ask uncomfortable questions."

I hear God calling me to use my privilege

And repent.

Those on the outside are now on the inside.

Jesus is calling,

For truth and reconciliation in this land

It's time to shake things up.

A good Christian is one who is prepared to resist.

Discussion Questions

Have you ever considered how your national identity shapes how you preach? Where do the illustrations for your sermon come from?

Do you believe national identity is an important concern in the book of Judges?

Are there ways you are both an insider and an outsider in your community?

Exercise

Write a sermon that deliberately centers on your nation.

5

Does anger have a place in my sermons?

ONE OF PREACHING'S PRIMARY functions is to apply the Bible in a local church. Persuasion plays an essential role in that process. One of the tools used to persuade is emotions. Yet when I started preaching, I remember thinking I didn't want people to judge me as too emotional. My impression was that women were perceived to be more emotional than men, and so they were dismissed. I wanted to be taken seriously, so I leaned into my intellectual side. But emotions are everywhere. Sometimes, I would see men express feelings when preaching, a slight tear in their eyes, and it moved people. I also saw men raising their voices, thundering at us, often calling for repentance for some sin. I couldn't imagine crying up in the front, let alone showing such anger. But sometimes, I felt such emotions when reading certain parts of the Bible. Spending six years reading these stories from the book of Judges produced some pretty strong feelings! I also struggle, very privately, with mild forms of anxiety and depression. There have been times when I wasn't in a good emotional space, but still, I would get up and preach and try to stop such emotions from leaking into my sermons. Or, as I discovered first-person sermons, I would allow myself to express emotion only when I was a character.

Lastly, there have been times when the church community has felt down or angry. There will come a time in the life of a church when there might be a complex pastoral crisis or challenge to navigate, and you will step up to preach, knowing there is a lot of feeling in the congregation. Do you ignore it? In this chapter, I want to explore the emotion of anger.

The expression of anger, particularly female anger, can feel jarring and out of place in many pulpits. I have begun to wrestle with how and when to express such anger. Is there a place for anger in evangelical preaching? And how do I convey such anger as a woman? To answer these questions, I will continue to learn from the feminist scholar Esther Fuchs, as well as other feminists, and their interpretation of Judges 16. I believe the more we can be real and develop a range of emotions when preaching, the more powerful our sermons can be.

Anger and the Text

As we saw in the last chapter, Fuchs argues that the Bible is seeking to teach truths about God and teaches women and men how to be women and men. Fuchs defines the masculinity portrayed in Judges 11 as strong and violent; I would add this is still true when it comes to Samson's story.[1] Men get angry. Samson is regularly angry, particularly at the Philistines. This has terrible consequences for women who frequently experience violence, not just from outsiders but also from their community. There has been a lot of analysis regarding Samson. He is sometimes described as a "man-child."[2] He represents the ideal strong and violent man, but he also makes impulsive decisions and never transitions into the role of father (which is part of the ancient Israelite rite of passage into adulthood).[3]

The story of Samson and Delilah is relatively well known. Yahweh gives Samson, a judge of Israel, extraordinary strength. A strength that comes from the length of his hair and the vows he has taken to commit himself to God. Yet Samson is wild and unpredictable, often having love affairs with the wrong sorts of women, leading him into trouble. Delilah is the third woman Samson engages with and whom the text says in Judges 16:4 that "he loves." The Philistines approach Delilah, wanting to know the secret of his strength and offering to pay Delilah if she can find out how to weaken him. She agrees, and then we see a series of attempts to find out. Finally, in verse 16, Samson gives in because of her "nagging." Delilah passes on that knowledge to the Philistines, and they capture Samson.

Delilah is one of the women who is named in the book of Judges. This is how the reader is introduced to her in Judges 16:4. Granted, it is from

1. Fuchs, *Feminist Theory*, 80.
2. Wilson, "Samson the Man-Child," 44.
3. Wilson, "Samson the Man-Child," 45–47.

Samson's point of view, but Exum notes that not only does Delilah have a name, but she is not linked to any patriarchal figure, implying she is an "independent woman."[4] This is seen as a positive for women today, but Smith suggests that it would not have been for the original hearers; people would view Delilah as "an object for pity."[5] Indeed, Klein assumes that Delilah is a "prostitute . . . a woman available to men."[6] One of the common observations by feminist scholars is that women fall into good and bad categories in the Bible. Delilah is seen to be a bad woman, and the first sign of this is her independence, followed by her willingness to betray Samson for money.

No motivation is given for why Delilah would do this or how she does it. It has been suggested she is a Philistine sympathizer, or a shrewd businesswoman, or even that a relative has died because of Samson, and she wants revenge.[7] Many have speculated and, in particular, often imagine how she seduces Samson into giving up his secrets. Kalmanofsky contends that the word in verse 5, "to persuade," has sexual undertones.[8] The classic image that comes to many people's minds when they reflect on Delilah is the "*femme fatale* . . . the woman is coded to represent the attraction and danger of female sexuality."[9] Similarly, Fuchs argues this is a recurring pattern: a "desirable wife-figure is particularly life-threatening to a passionate husband-figure."[10] Kalmanofsky goes even further, suggesting that a common theme throughout the book of Judges is the danger of women who try to "control or overpower men;" there is a warning that when women (such as Delilah or earlier Jael) use their power, it results in "bad things that lead to violence."[11] Although the same comment could be made regarding men—when they seek to control women, it leads to their deaths. Smith believes that feminists often want to either redeem Delilah, turn a negative portrayal into a positive one, or condemn the Bible as unredeemably misogynistic.[12] That desire for simplicity is something preachers will be tempted to do as well, but people are never that simple.

4. Exum, *Plotted, Shot, and Painted*, 181.

5. Smith, "Delilah," 110.

6. Klein, *Triumph of Irony*, 120.

7. Japinga, *Preaching the Women*, Delilah.

8. Kalmanofsky, *Gender-Play*, 83.

9. Exum, *Plotted, Shot, and Painted*, 176

10. Fuchs, *Sexual Politics*, 148.

11. Kalmanofsky, *Gender-Play*, 71.

12. Smith, "Delilah," 114.

As an evangelical female preacher, reading Fuchs and other feminist scholars has challenged me to ask hard questions about how much patriarchal ideology I have absorbed through reading the Bible and then which I unintentionally promote. For Fuchs, women serve in the biblical text as "symbolic reproducers of the nation . . . disseminators of its values."[13] As an evangelical preacher, I am both a passive participant and an active producer of the evangelical culture and tradition I work in. The temptation for an evangelical female preacher is to smooth away the difficulties in the biblical text and keep everything calm and happy. Do not show too much anger or distress. Evangelicals will most likely default to criticizing Delilah.[14]

The Preacher and Anger

Pathos, or in other words, emotions, should play a role in preaching.[15] MacBride outlines how ancient rhetorical practice emphasized the importance of emotions when it came to oral communication because speakers like Aristotle understood that emotions "initiate deliberation and provoke action."[16] They are essential to the art of persuasion. However, many evangelicals in Australia can feel uncomfortable or suspicious of preachers who display too much feeling.[17] Mitchell suggests that this uncomfortableness comes from the West's tendency to separate the body from our soul. We dismiss our bodies and, therefore, our feelings.[18] This can be a particular struggle for women. Gross noticed after working and training many female preachers how many of them "were disconnected from their bodies," resulting in faltering voices.[19] Gross provides concrete, practical advice for women to discover their voices, including saying different lines in different emotional tones out loud.[20] Every sermon will have some emotional

---

13. Fuchs, *Feminist Theory*, 97. Fuchs draws on Yuval-Davis's work here. See Yuval-Davis et al., *Woman–Nation–State*, 7–10.

14. Webb notes that Delilah's name is similar to the name "night" in Hebrew, suggesting she is like "darkness" which will close in on Samson, "another trap" from the Philistines. See Webb, *Book of Judges*, 398.

15. Arthurs, "Place of Pathos," 15.

16. MacBride, *Catching the Wave*, 146.

17. Raiter, "On Sermons and Preaching," 76.

18. Mitchell, "Emotion and Preaching," 26.

19. Gross, *Women's Voices*, 46–47.

20. Gross, *Women's Voices*, 120–21.

impact, even if a preacher gives no thought to it. Yet if a preacher wants those listening to care about the biblical text or the implications of that text, they need to show listeners "why the speaker cares."[21] I think this is particularly relevant when dealing with Old Testament texts. Sometimes, I will get someone to read the biblical story before I preach, and when it's a hard story like many in the book of Judges, you can almost hear the question in the air: why are we looking at this text? Part of my job is to demonstrate how even though a text might seem irrelevant or awful, there is richness, and God's grace can still be found.

A preacher can prepare by reflecting and shaping the emotional impact they hope their listeners will feel. Mitchell encourages preachers to ground their sermons in real life and aim to finish them with the "ecstatic reinforcement of the biblical text and its behavioral purpose."[22] One of the decisions I made early on when preaching this story was to keep my focus on Delilah and Samson. Samson's story begins a few chapters before Delilah is introduced, and there is a range of other things happening in this broader story, including his interactions with other women. Still, I stayed just with this one relationship to keep the emotions tight and raw.

While many preachers agree that feelings are important, the emotion of anger can be problematic for evangelicals. This is because anger can be seen as sinful and to be avoided. It can be viewed as destructive.[23] There is anger that can come out of a preacher that signals unhealth. There could be personal anger that the preacher is unaware of and has not dealt with.[24] Perhaps in frustration at the congregation, the preacher lashes out without love. This needs to be checked and dealt with by seeing a psychologist or mentor or having some form of supervisor. Preachers need to be held to account. There is no place for spiritual abuse in the church.[25]

---

21. Hogan and Reid, *Connecting with the Congregation*, 79.

22. Mitchell, "Emotion and Preaching," 28.

23. Keefe, "Tending the Fire of Anger," 68. Cooper, writing a personal piece for the Gospel Coalition, comments about how her anger was a sin causing havoc in her marriage. While anger can be unhelpful there is no acknowledgment of how it could also be positive. See Cooper, "Wrath of Jodie."

24. Wardlaw, "Preaching from Anger."

25. The popular podcast *The Rise and Fall of Mars Hill* exposes the dangers when unhealthy anger and abuse is left unchecked. See *The Rise and Fall of Mars Hill*. Also see Kruger's work that explores the impact of spiritual abuse and how churches can do things differently, in his *Bully Pulpit*.

Today, many listeners are looking for vulnerability. I have sought to be vulnerable in my sermons, and I think it can be powerful but also dangerous and potentially harmful. I remember when I first started preaching, disclosing personal matters in part so I could relate particularly to young people and in part because I was angry, and there was something powerful about voicing my anger to a bunch of strangers. I have needed to wrestle and continue to wrestle with the ethical implications of sharing particularly when it involves other people. Even in this sample sermon, while I do not go into the details of any relationship, I hint at some of the tensions I have faced. On the one hand, this can be permission-giving for others listening, to know they are not alone as they might be going through similar things. On the other hand, I am talking about real people whom I deeply care about but who might not want matters to be so publicly discussed. Lovell and Richardson explore this tension. Preachers can operate between the public and private domains, seeking to integrate both spaces as they bring the private into the public domain to those listening.[26] This allows a preacher to address real challenges people are facing. For example, I am open about my questions and struggles:

> I thought when I was younger that to be a wife meant to be stuck doing all the household chores, so I crawled into the single box. It's hard to occupy the femme fatal box if you are a Christian. Female sexuality is just kind of denied, so I crawled into the single box and stayed there for a long time, but then you meet someone, and the walls collapse. So, Delilah is with Samson, and Samson loves her, but again, what about Delilah? Maybe she's not sure. Maybe some days she loves Samson, but other days she finds herself playing the housewife, cooking his dinners, organizing him, cleaning up his shit, and thinking to herself, I didn't think this would be me.

One of the roles of preachers is to provide resources to their congregation by showing them that they are grappling with similar issues.[27] It resonates particularly with people shaped by our postmodern context who are likely to relate to preachers who share "stories and life experiences."[28]

The line between private and public is a challenge for not just preachers, but artists and writers as well. There is a blurring of lines in fiction with a whole genre known as auto-fiction. It is defined as when an author "blends

26. Lovell and Richardson, *Sustaining Preachers and Preaching*, 49.

27. Lovell and Richardson, *Sustaining Preachers and Preaching*, 77–78.

28. Johnston, *Preaching to a Postmodern World*, 78.

the autobiographical and the fictional."[29] It's exciting but can cause anger and hurt. One writer, Hjorth, seemingly hinted at some dark secrets about her family in her book *Will and Testament*.[30] Her family then cut her off and wrote their own book. Hjorth followed up her novel with a second book exploring what it's like to be a daughter cut off from her mother.[31] One of the ways a preacher will be sustained long term is to have a strong network of relationships at both the private and public level and, of course, fostering a strong relationship with God as well.[32] In these close relationships, there are people a preacher can go to for discernment in these matters.

Alongside vulnerability, another popular trait today is authenticity. One of the rhetorical techniques a preacher can use is to find common ground with our listeners; this is why identification can be so powerful.[33] Swears defines authenticity as not just being someone that people can identify with, but a preacher should be someone that people see is trying to follow Christ authentically, not just when they speak but in the rest of their weeks.[34] This is the strength of the local pastor as opposed to an itinerant preacher. Along similar lines, Peterson argues that for authenticity to be a virtue, it needs to be grounded in both honesty and for Christians learning to conform ourselves into the image of Christ.[35] While I agree, I would add in order to grow in the fruit of the spirit, as Paul describes in Galatians, there needs to be space to process our anger first.

Not all anger is bad. In fact, according to Keefe, there are many people in our wider society, like psychologists and activists, who view anger positively. Anger can illuminate and generate something "creative" and new by "challenging structures of injustice."[36] Perhaps this is why some evangelicals could be uncomfortable with anger: they don't want the systems to change. Not only are many evangelicals uncomfortable with anger, but this discomfort only increases when it comes to women expressing anger. An

---

29. Egan and Kearney, "How Autofiction Turns the Personal into the Political."

30. Hjorth, *Will and Testament*.

31. Hjorth, *Is Mother Dead?*

32. Lovell and Richardson, *Sustaining Preachers and Preaching*, 51.

33. Hogan and Reid, *Connecting with the Congregation*, 78.

34. Swears, *Preaching to Head and Heart*, 40–41.

35. Peterson, *Where Goodness Still Grows*.

36. Keefe, "Tending the Fire of Anger," 68. Traister explores how women's anger have changed society for the better, saying we need to tell their stories more. See Traister, *Good and Mad*.

angry woman is traditionally viewed as a negative, with many denigratory labels used to describe women when they are angry—including "bitch" or "harpy."[37] Women already struggle to use their voices in the evangelical church and so can avoid expressing anger to be accepted. Gross explores the gender norms taught in churches that can render women mute. She argues that even if women are allowed to speak, they have often been trained "to be nice and kind, calm and quiet," which can disconnect them from their real feelings and experiences.[38] Anger is not seen as a good persuasive tool for evangelical women. As Gross talked to women and taught them how to preach, she noticed how many felt deeply uncomfortable in their bodies.[39] I identify with these words and have been on a journey to discovering the full range of my preaching voice. One of the ways a preacher can do that is to try what might feel like a new voice or perhaps a new range in your own voice. Reid cautions that care should be taken when trying something new as this could be jarring for listeners familiar with the way you already speak.[40] It requires small changes. For example, as I mentioned earlier, I started experimenting with anger when I created narrative sermons and then moved to expressing it as me.

I believe we can learn much from other, often more marginalized, women about using anger. Womanism is a sister of feminism but considers how racism and social status affect a woman's experience. Austin Channing Brown is one incredible preacher I have heard in recent years who speaks from this perspective.[41] Her sermons have clarity and voice anger for the injustice perpetrated today. Similarly, Curtice, a Potawatomi woman, grapples with what it means to be a Christian and an Indigenous woman in the US. She asks whether we can go to church even if we are angry that the church has been implicated in many "oppressive acts" against women and Indigenous people.[42] Her answer is yes, anger is needed, and Indigenous people cannot wait for "the church to give us permission."[43] She resolves to keep walking and speaking into this difficult space, asking hard questions

37. Keefe, "Tending the Fire of Anger," 69; Ashcroft et al., *Empire Writes Back*.

38. Gross, *Women's Voices*, 72.

39. Gross, *Women's Voices*, 48–58.

40. Reid, *Four Voices of Preaching*, 205.

41. One influential sermon I listened to is about Rizpah. See Brown, "Climbing the Mountain of Injustice."

42. Curtice, *Native*, 104.

43. Curtice, *Native*, 104.

and recognizing that "anger and hope are colaborers."[44] I have been inspired to take hold of some of the anger that these women convey.

As I sat with this troubling story in Judges 16, I could hear angry rumblings of women again marching on our streets. Women have been marching and trying to use their voices for a long time in the public square. Sometimes, they are angry. I would say rightly angry. Woollacott and Staff write that women are angry because of a "lack of equal rights, their treatment by governments, and issues surrounding sex."[45] Women respond angrily as they recognize how patriarchy still lingers and damages them. One response I read from a woman who was deeply moved by Delilah's story was by Wurtzel. She recalls seeing Delilah as a hero when she was a teenager. This is partly because she can see women beaten down by the circumstances of their lives around her, so it was refreshing to see a woman who seemed confident.[46] This was Wurtzel's initial interest, but the more she thought about Delilah, the more she could see her story addressing women's complicated feelings in our relationships. The back-and-forth dialogue between Samson and Delilah reveals how daunting it can be to be vulnerable in a relationship because it requires both people to "relinquish" some of their power and trust the other person.[47] For Delilah and Samson, the opposite happens with the Bible recording for us the "first ever incident of intimate terrorism."[48] I resonated with these words because they articulated feelings I was trying to process. I was trying to navigate through a romantic relationship. I had found myself both angry and in love, struggling to know myself in this relationship and feeling these gendered expectations fall on me. The Whiteheads address the emotion of anger in their book, naming intimate anger as the most common place we process anger and sometimes the most damaging place because we end up attacking people who know our weaknesses. They propose that "maturity brings us to recognize anger as intimacy's inevitable companion—and even part of its strength."[49] Of course, for this to happen, people need to learn how to work through anger in healthy ways, not destructive ways. Sometimes, there is an overlap between public anger, like seeing women protesting against injustice, and

44. Curtice, *Native*, 104.

45. Woollacott and Staff, "Sex, Power and Anger."

46. I include her quote in my sermon.

47. Wurtzel, *Bitch*, 53.

48. Wurtzel, *Bitch*, 52.

49. Whitehead and Whitehead, *Transforming Our Painful Emotions*, 39.

intimate anger. Keizer analyzes ancient stories of women's anger written by male authors. We can see how women's anger often "derives from an imbalance that is never entirely internal."[50] I decided to explore this in the sermon because I believe many others are struggling with this, but it's not often discussed in a church setting.

Anger and the Listener

The purpose of application in preaching is to connect a biblical text to those listening and show how it is relevant.[51] The hope is that listeners might recognize they are hearing God's Word and be moved to respond.[52] According to Doriani, the goal of application is to "lead people to know God and conform themselves" to God.[53] Good application should be "holistic," addressing all aspects of a person.[54] As the church listens, God's purposes are applied and lived out.[55] Lane suggests that there is a close relationship between application and persuasion. Persuasion, according to Lane, "calls for change in accord with the text's application."[56] Broadus goes further, arguing that "application" is better understood as "persuasion."[57] One strategy a preacher can use to apply the biblical text and persuade the listener is by engaging the emotions. When a preacher feels and expresses such feelings it often deeply impacts those listening.[58] This is what people will remember: the feeling. Preaching that relies on reason forgets what neuroscience has needed to remind us of—people use both their heads and hearts.[59] Part of what it means to be human is to feel.

50. Keizer, *Enigma of Anger*, 168.

51. Webb, *Old Texts, New Sermons*, 36; Thompson, *Preaching Biblically*, 51. Capill describes it as pressing the biblical truth onto the lives of our listeners. See Capill, *Heart Is the Target*, 30. Broadus defines application when a preacher shows "how the subject applies to the person addressed." See Broadus, *Preparation and Delivery*, 211; Buttrick, *Homiletic*, 33.

52. Ortberg, "Biblical Preaching Is About Life Change," 452.

53. Doriani, *Putting Truth to Work*, 39.

54. Griffith, "Dangerous Edge."

55. Holt and Spears, "Ecclesia as Primary Context," 72–73.

56. Lane, "Application and Persuasion," 57.

57. Broadus, *Preparation and Delivery*, 215.

58. Kuruvilla, *Manual for Preaching*, 151.

59. Kuruvilla, *Manual for Preaching*, 151.

In our contemporary context, anger is an appropriate persuasive tool because it connects with many women's anger in our culture. Buechner writes that a preacher must "always try to feel what it is like to live inside the skins of the people" they are preaching to.[60] In light of reports into domestic violence in the church, Baird critiques the church's response, asking, "Where is the urgency, the garment-tearing, the rage, shame, fury and thunder" in the pulpits?[61] If our preaching fails to address women's anger and stays silent and positive, it denies the injustices still afflicting women. One way forward is for evangelical preachers to acknowledge that biblical texts can anger us. I get frustrated when I read the Judges 16 narrative and see that the story is told entirely from Samson's view, and I am left to wonder what Delilah's version of events would be. Stephens and McCallum suggest that whenever we retell a story, we reproduce or contest the particular ideology in the text. There is the potential for a "new negotiation between the already given and the new."[62] Buechner, musing on the power of truth, describes truth not just as a fact—it delves into emotions, and a good preacher is able to dare to name and speak into the times, whatever they might be: "one wonders if there is anything more crucial for the preacher to do that to obey the sadness of our times," or we might say the "anger of our times" because it's often only by naming what is real and hard that people can then hear the good news of God's grace.[63] Many female writers have been pursuing this recently—taking familiar figures or tales and making the women in these more visible. For example, Anna Funder explores the life of Eileen O'Shaughnessy (George Orwell's wife) and how her story intersects with modern-day concerns about being a wife. Funder addresses the gap that still exists today, with many women still carrying the bulk of household work. To be a wife is a "life and death struggle between maintaining herself, and the self-sacrifice and self-effacement so lauded of women in patriarchy."[64] That tug-of-war is addressed in my sample sermon.

When I preached on Judges 16, I wanted to experiment with the use of anger. One of the phrases that caught my attention was Wurtzel musing on an old folk song about Samson and Delilah. The song's focus was Samson "tearing down the walls," but Wurtzel, contemplating her unexpressed

---

60. Buechner, *Telling the Truth*, 8.

61. Baird, "Church Stripped Bare."

62. Stephens and McCallum, "Pre-Texts, Metanarratives."

63. Buechner, *Telling the Truth*, 9.

64. Funder, *Wifedom*, 54.

anger, started to wonder about Delilah: "what if she wanted to tear things down?"[65] That line connected with me, and I had the beginnings of a sermon. I often use a recurring phrase or motif in my sermons. This is a rhetorical strategy in oral communication. It helps me, as a preacher, remember and not rely on notes when preaching; hopefully, listeners will remember, too. I used the phrase "tearing down the walls" to explore my anger and vulnerabilities about what it means to be a woman in a relationship. I want to tear down some of the stereotypes surrounding Delilah. In the sermon, I wanted to interrogate and expand upon the picture of Delilah as the "bad girl." We can interrogate biblical stories by reading all Scripture in light of Jesus. Jesus was both compassionate and showed anger in response to injustice. Jesus, in his life, death, and resurrection, opened up a new way to live. He turned things upside down as he worked towards justice, peace, and reconciliation with all people to Godself.

I should sound a note of caution and recognize it can be easy to assume that everyone will respond to the text as I do. There will still be a range of differences even in a congregation that might attract similar-minded people. When a preacher decides to focus on women, particularly if you show anger, you need to be aware that some people might feel uncomfortable or even fundamentally disagree. Jeter and Allen discuss the importance of relationships between the preacher and the congregation. There needs to be a "strong and trusted pastoral relationship;" this will create a willingness in both the preacher and the congregation to listen to one another even when it might be difficult.[66]

Another potential objection to the use of anger or even the decision to focus on the personal dynamics in Delilah and Samson's relationship might seem to many evangelical preachers to be stepping out of the boundaries of what a sermon should be about. As I have noted earlier, many evangelical preachers are rightly Christ-centred and gospel-focused. That means, typically, what Jesus did on the cross should be mentioned, if not be the central message.[67] Some evangelical homileticians critique the "anthropocentric emphasis" in contemporary preaching and call for a more God-centred approach.[68] I might at this point be parting with many evangelicals, but I believe that part of the gospel, the good news, is that God is interested in all

65. Wurtzel, Bitch, 86.

66. Jeter Jr. and Allen, One Gospel, Many Ears, 171.

67. Chapell, Christ-Centered Preaching.

68. Paquarello, Christian Preaching, 14–15.

aspects of our lives and this world. As a preacher, we can talk about a whole range of topics, including relationship dynamics and emotions, but with a theological distinctiveness. Strawn writes about one of the Old Testament's gifts is honesty. The people of Israel's record in the book of Judges testifies to how real and ugly both the world and faith can be.[69] Doing this opens the way for God to come and bring healing and reconciliation.

Conclusion

Preaching aims to apply the biblical text to the contemporary context. There are difficult stories in the Bible for many women, who are unsure how to respond to them. Challenges and injustices for women in our society also need to be wrestled with. I believe anger can be a persuasive tool to address both realities. Yet anger, particularly female anger, can be stifled in the church. We must help women bring their whole selves to preaching, including anger. Feminist scholars can facilitate such a space because they often name the troubling parts of the Bible like those we have seen when briefly examining the story of Delilah. Anger can be powerful if we engage with our emotions healthily, leading to justice, healing, and a positive change for all.

Sample Sermon

Can we tear down the walls this morning and be real for a moment? I know we all have our public selves and our private selves, and while hopefully there is a lot of overlap between the two, there can also be a separation we maintain. There are many things we don't know about one another, even people we are close with, like our friends. If I were to tear a wall down for you, I would show you a woman on the side of the road at night, frustrated with her boyfriend. That woman would be me. Surprise! I never thought I'd be that woman. Who knew? I'm a calm, independent woman, that's been me my whole life, well, maybe not the calm part, but definitely the single part. But after COVID and the lockdown, I wanted to tear the walls down on my safety box and give dating a go, so I went online. And what I discovered, which I'm sure many of you have also experienced, is that romantic relationships are both beautiful and fraught. When you are in

---

69. Strawn, *Honest to God Preaching*, chapter 1.

such a close relationship with someone, it can feel like all the walls are coming down and you are exposed. No wonder we keep so much of this private. It's not always pretty.

But that's what the book of Judges is inviting us into—the walls are down, and in Judges 16, we are entering the private realm, into the complicated dynamics of a romantic couple, Samson and Delilah. It's not always pretty, so maybe that's why people have tried to reduce or oversimplify the story. It doesn't help that this story in our Bibles is told primarily from the perspective of the man, Samson. Does anyone else get frustrated by this? We follow Samson, falling in and out of love with women, and here he is once more loving a woman in the valley of Sorek. At least this time, we have a name. The woman is Delilah. Delilah, now she is a woman boxed in our imaginations, isn't she? She's the femme fatale, seductress, betrayer, a warning for all men. That's her public persona popping up in countless artworks and songs: her breasts hanging out, red lipstick on, dangling a pair of scissors in her hands. But this seems to be more fantasy than reality.

So, let's try and tear down these walls around her. For starters, it seems like Delilah might have been a single, independent woman. That's the first striking thing about her. Her father's name or her husband's doesn't appear. It's just her, well, her and Samson, their names wrapped together, but before Samson wandered into the Valley of Sorek, there was just Delilah. It sounds pretty cool; she's a role model for all the independent women out there today, but it may not have felt so cool in Delilah's day. Without a man, she is in a potentially precarious position. I wonder what she wants? Does she want to be single, or does she want to be married? Maybe she is divided. I am. I thought when I was younger that to be a wife meant to be stuck doing all the household chores and so I crawled into the single box (it's hard to occupy the femme fatal box if you are a Christian; female sexuality is just kind of denied) and stayed there for a long time, but then you meet someone and the walls collapse. So, Delilah is with Samson, and Samson loves her, but again, what about Delilah? Maybe she's not sure. Maybe some days she loves Samson, but other days she finds herself playing the housewife, cooking his dinners, organizing him, cleaning up his shit, and thinking to herself, I didn't think this would be me. I'm not that type of woman. And if I'm going to be that type, why won't you marry me? Don't you think I could be your wife? Maybe she is tired and frustrated when there is a knock on her door and this offer is made to her:

*The lords of the Philistines came to her and said to her, "Coax him,
and find out what makes his strength so great, and how we may
overpower him, so that we may bind him in order to subdue him;
and we will each give you eleven hundred pieces of silver."*[70]

Is Delilah a woman who sells out her man? It seems like it. The Philistines have been trying for years to defeat Samson. He is an Israelite;
they hate the Israelites, and the Israelites hate the Philistines. They are
enemies at war against one another. But lately, Samson has had the upper
hand. He is so strong, ripping lions apart with his bare hands. He even
dared to take one of their women and marry her. So, they tried to use her
and went to her with a similar offer. But Samson ends up tearing those
Philistines to pieces, killing thirty men in anger before returning to his
parents' home. He leaves his wife behind. Her father gives her to another
man, which makes Samson so mad that he kills three hundred foxes and
uses them as torches, burning flesh in the night. He lets them go howling.
They run through grainfields so everything catches on fire, and it all burns
down. The Philistines, furious at such destruction, take Samson's wife and
her father and burn them in retaliation. Men muster from both sides to
battle, but nobody can stop Samson, not even ropes. Using the jawbone of
a donkey, Samson hits and hits, striking down a thousand men.

The Philistines are angry. They want revenge. That's why they are coming to Delilah. They want to bring Samson down, but they can't do it publicly
on the battlefield, so they strike what they think is his weak spot: women.
Women, they make men do crazy things, isn't that what they say? Find out
his strength, Delilah, by any means necessary, and we will each give you
eleven hundred pieces of silver. I understand the Philistines and where they
are coming from, but why does Delilah agree? Is she a Philistine? Has Samson once more fallen in love with the enemy? Her name is of Hebrew origin,
but the valley of Sorek is kind of caught in the middle between these two
nations. She lives in a war zone. Presumably, she knows then what it is to
be unsafe, always on edge to whatever might happen next. Presumably, she
knows who Samson is. Has he told her the stories of his triumphs, trying to
impress her? What does she think about the fact that he left his wife and she
burned? Is this how he shows love? Is she angry to be put in this position,
caught in the middle between these warring groups? The Philistines suggest
she seduce Samson. That's the box they put her in. You're attractive. You're
a woman. Use your womanly charms. That's what we picture her doing,

70. Judg 16:5 (NRSV).

stroking his muscles, his ego, flirting with him, having sex, and then when he's spent asking the question. Although that's complete conjecture. The text doesn't tell us where they are, it just rather plainly says:

> So, Delilah said to Samson, "Please tell me what makes your strength so great, and how you could be bound, so that one could subdue you."[71]

Delilah is direct. It's not subtle at all. She just comes up and asks Samson: "Tell me what makes you strong and how someone could defeat you." Both lie to one another in this moment. Delilah omits that the Philistines have come to her offering money, and Samson makes up a story about his strength, if seven fresh bowstrings that have been dried are bound around him he will become weak. Delilah tests his words, binding him with these bowstrings and then shouting, "The Philistines are upon you, Samson!" The bonds snap easily, the lies collapse around them both, but neither says a word. There's no acknowledgment, at least on the surface.

The walls are down, and we see how hard it is to communicate, to build trust. Have you ever found yourself struggling to say what you really feel? Maybe you conceal, omit, or add, embellish, and your partner notices. They become angry, although maybe the anger is not visible, they keep the thought to themselves, but it's there: you lied, you lied to me! Suddenly, every word is turned over and examined. Hurtful words are stored up and remembered. He said this, he promised me this, but he didn't come through. He's unreliable. She's not trustworthy. She let me down. And underneath anger: it's what I have always feared. I can't be completely myself before them. He doesn't know me at all. He doesn't know what pressures I'm facing. The words cut back and forth between Delilah and Samson, almost like a game. When you know someone well, you know how to hurt them. You learn where they are weak and what they are sensitive to. Now, there is mistrust and anger. We watch in on this very private conversation along with the narrator and God. It's not pretty but it's real.

> Then Delilah said to Samson, "You have mocked me and told me lies; please tell me how you could be bound."[72]

Delilah is more forceful the second time. But it makes no difference. Samson spins a story about new ropes being the key. She takes new ropes and wraps them around him, shouts, "Philistines coming!," and he breaks

71. Judg 16:6 (NRSV).

72. Judg 16:10 (NRSV).

free. Again, she asks, and again, he spins a fanciful story about seven locks of his hair, if plaited together, will make him weak. Does Samson know what's she up to? Or is he so obsessed with himself, so confident in his strength and clever answers, that he can't even see her as a full person? Isn't she there just to listen to him? Give him all the support and encouragement he needs? She grounds him. She makes him a better man. He likes having her by his side. He wants others to see them together. He never asks about her life or thoughts or dreams.

Just ask me a question about myself! Maybe that is what Delilah wants to shout. She is trying to work out if Samson really does love her, all of her. He says he loves me, but how can he? I'm his fantasy. He's put me a box, the nice woman, there to meet all his needs, but I'm more than that. When you first meet someone, you are on your best behavior, right? There's a haze, a rush to falling in love. It can actually take a while to see the actual person you are with and not just the one you have constructed in your head. Most of us are not just one thing, right? Sometimes, the Bible gets accused of putting women into boxes. Good women are wives and mothers, virgin daughters. Obedient, nurturing, supporting their man. Bad women are foreign, whores, violent, and manipulative. There's a fear, it seems, hovering in the book of Judges, with some men suspecting that all women will be their downfall. It's kind of laughable because it's actually women who tend to suffer at the hands of men, stripped of opportunities and agency, stripped of their voice, sometimes violently killed and discarded. Here is Delilah, reduced to a few words on a page, but behind those words, there is a real complicated person, just like Samson. I am nice and not nice; I want to be loved, and I don't want to love. I get angry, so angry that sometimes I wish I could tear down the walls with my bare hands. Sometimes, I get so angry that I hit myself, or I deliberately start a fight. Sometimes I am a bitch. Will you love me then? I am tearing down the walls and showing you who I am, and it's not all pretty.

> Then she said to him, "How can you say, 'I love you,' when your heart is not with me? You have mocked me three times now and have not told me what makes your strength so great." Finally, after she had nagged him with her words day after day, and pestered him, he was tired to death.[73]

73. Judg 16:15–16 (NRSV).

She nagged him. Classic woman, right? Forget the seduction. It's the nagging that gets Samson in the end. She just keeps going on and on, so demanding, and he can't bear to hear another word! This will shut her up. Give her the truth, and then she'll leave you alone. Maybe it's seeing how easy it is for him to move about in the world that makes her angry. She can't do that. She can't just walk wherever she wants, do whatever she wants. Why can't she tear down walls like Samson? Scream and lose control? She has all this anger; she doesn't even know from where, but it's just there building, and she doesn't know what to do with it. Wurtzel writes that she loved Delilah when she was a teenager because:

> I lived in a world of exhausted, taxed single mothers at the mercy of men who overworked and underpaid them, men who forgot to send child-support checks, men who forgot they had children . . . I had never in my life encountered a woman who'd brought a man down. Until Delilah.[74]

It's strange for Delilah to be seen as a hero. And I'm not sure if she is a hero, but neither am I sure she is the villain. Those boxes are too simple. These boxes are what can drive us to tear it all down. Samson tells her, shave my hair off, and my strength will go. He gives her his heart, and she breaks it. She brings a man in, and he shaves Samson's hair off while she holds him down, and just like that, he is depleted. The Philistines burst in and seize him, tear out his eyes, bind him in bronze shackles, and take him away. That's the end of Samson and Delilah.

Does Delilah play out that moment again and again? Or does she put it into a little box and move on? They've broken up, and that's that. Are there traces of Samson that she comes across in her house? Strands of hair and clothes left behind? Does she feel regret? God doesn't appear directly in this story, and we can wonder what this has to do with our faith. I think this story tears the walls down and gives us a glimpse into a private relationship, showing how those we love can hurt us. I don't think this is a model relationship we should be aspiring to, but maybe it helps us to examine our relationships, our own complicated feelings, and how hard it is to trust and communicate and love someone else, let alone God. Can we come as we are to God? Walls down, even when we are angry or not sure who we are or who we want to be. I'd like to think yes. I'd like to think God can take it. Can you let your walls down? Is something bothering

---

74. Wurtzel, *Bitch*, 44.

you, making you angry, perhaps in your relationship, or perhaps as you look out on the world, can you be real with God? Maybe you'll need to shout. You can bring it to God, but don't let it build and build until you find yourself in shackles and don't know how to break free. Jesus comes to redeem and transform all of our emotions and relationships.

Discussion Questions

Do you think emotions have a place in preaching? Including anger?

When have you experienced a strong emotional reaction to a sermon (or a biblical text)?

Can a sermon still be a Christian sermon if Christ is not mentioned?

Exercise

Practice your sermon out loud before you deliver it, and experiment with different tones, pitches, and body stances. Notice what emotions you are trying to convey.

6

Should women be the only ones
to tell women's stories?

As I started experimenting more with first-person narrative sermonic structures, I mostly focused on amplifying female voices. Still, I have also inhabited and told the stories of male characters from the Bible. That can be just as provocative, inhabiting the powerful, placing myself in the role of a king or a prophet. One day, I was teaching a homiletics class, and a man asked, "Can men inhabit and give voice to female characters?" I have to confess I had never seen a man do this before, leading me to reflect on the discussion about appropriation happening in our broader Western culture. There has been criticism and debate in recent years about who can tell what stories. I suspect that appropriation is not something many preachers give much attention to. Yet, I believe there could be value in recognizing how preachers appropriate biblical stories and bring them into the contemporary context. I want to explore this question by looking at the story of the Levite's concubine in Judges 19.

Appropriation and the Preacher

There is a conversation on appropriation happening in the broader Western culture. Book deals have been criticized. For example, in 2020, Jeanine Cummins's book *American Dirt* was criticized by some Latinx authors for stereotyping Mexicans. There was also frustration that publishers had chosen to elevate a white woman's voice rather than publish a Latinx author.[1] Movie deals have collapsed, and actors have pulled out of films when accused of appropriating transgender people's stories. Halle Berry had almost signed on to play a transgender woman, but after a backlash from the transgender community, she withdrew from the role.[2] Actors and directors are discussing whether straight actors can play LGBTQI+ characters.[3] The author Lionel Shriver gave a controversial speech in 2016 at Brisbane's Writer's Festival, where she warned that appropriation was creating fear amongst artists and authors. She lamented that this fear could lead to the end of fiction or fiction that is so "hedged, so circumscribed, so tippy-toe, that we'd indeed be better off not writing the anodyne drivel to begin with."[4] Appropriation asks questions about who has the power and authority to tell what stories.

Appropriation, in its simplest sense, is when people in a "dominant culture take from the culture of marginalised communities, resulting in some harm of offense."[5] Bucar traces the development of this term back to the 1920s when Black scholars raised questions around representations of African Americans in popular books like *Brer Rabbit*.[6] Bucar goes on to argue that scholars have not given religious appropriation proper consideration. This is partly due to a liberal secular West that separates spirituality from religion and tends to believe that being spiritual is the superior choice.[7] There are many examples of appropriation by individuals who customize and choose what spiritual practices they want to take up. This leaves religion as something that can be discarded and disregarded. Yet, Bucar suggests such an approach can be quite harmful and offensive to those committed to particular religious traditions. Appropriation generally focuses on outsiders borrowing or stealing from another community, but Bucar stresses appropriation can also happen within communities. Religious communities are diverse, meaning individuals have different experiences and reactions that must be considered. One of the primary ethical concerns that needs to

1. Flood, "Publishers Defend American Dirt."
2. Moreau, "Halle Berry Pulls Out of Transgender Film."
3. Compton, "Should Straight Actors Still Play Gay Characters?"
4. Shriver, "Lionel Shriver's Full Speech."
5. Bucar, *Stealing My Religion*, 5.
6. Bucar, *Stealing My Religion*, 4.
7. Bucar, *Stealing My Religion*, 26.

be asked is who is harmed or exploited by appropriation.[8] This should be a concern for Christians. A primary Christian ethic is a concern and love for others, particularly those who are vulnerable. Christians also have a long history of appropriation. Preachers must be willing to reflect on any harm done by what stories we draw on and who tells those stories.

Christian preachers have long appropriated the Jewish Scriptures. This is not always fully recognized or acknowledged especially in the local church, but there is still a discussion about the legitimacy of this move in academic circles. Matthew argues that New Testament writers followed Jesus "creatively reading" what were their Scriptures "in light of the Christ event."[9] Early church theologians would follow suit but would no longer be Jewish. Figures such as Clement argued that the Jewish texts are Christian texts, stating that "Judaism was a preliminary form of Christianity."[10] This is signaled by the name Christians give the Hebrew Bible—it is known as the Old Testament, giving the impression that these texts are irrelevant in some way. Jewish scholars have commented on such statements' adverse effects on their communities. This pattern of appropriation has, at times, caused harm and given rise to a long history of antisemitism by Christians, which must continue to be acknowledged, repented, and worked through.

Sometimes, Christians will be tempted when addressing the violence in the Old Testament or the lack of women in the biblical text to suggest this was solved by Christ, thus implying that the Jewish religion is backward and primitive compared to Christianity.[11] I have been guilty of this at times. Some feminist scholars can come to the Bible and see nothing good for women.[12] Stanton judges the Jewish customs and laws as inferior to the customs and laws of her day.[13] She briefly mentions the Levite's concubine, saying how terrible the story is before adding, "There are many instances in the Old Testament where women have been thrown to the mob, like a bone to dogs," and this results with women suffering today because people learn

8. Bucar, *Stealing My Religion*, 28.

9. Matthew, "'All That the Prophets Have Declared,'" xii.

10. Bushur, "Early Christian Appropriation," 73.

11. Levine, "When the Bible Becomes Weaponized."

12. Amador, "Feminist Biblical Hermeneutics," 43.

13. Fuchs, *Feminist Theory*, 73. Stanton, it is true, does write out of her context and refers to the idea that women and men have "natural, inalienable rights," which the daughter in this story is "ignorant" of. She wishes the daughter had rebelled. However, I believe that this wish is speaking again to Stanton's context; she wishes more women would rebel and fight for their rights in her day too. See Stanton, *Woman's Bible*, 21.

this from the Bible which is "so revered."[14] Some feminist scholars are suspicious of other feminist scholars who believe the Bible is not completely bad news for women. They believe such scholars say this to maintain their religious convictions. But perhaps their presuppositions are also at play. They come convinced that religion is wrong. Fuchs argues that theological feminism and what she calls "academic" feminism sometimes have an "antagonistic relationship," but she proposes that a form of dialogue "in the tradition of feminist quilting" could be more enriching for both sides.[15] Since World War II, there have been moves to bring Jewish and Christian interpreters into dialogue and have them learn from one another.[16] Many academics will now try to refer to the Old Testament texts as the Hebrew Bible. However, in my experience, this distinction is primarily made in the academy rather than a local church. Levine suggests Christians need to be honest and admit the "supersessionist impulse" of our religion.[17] She adds that Judaism also contains this impulse. As Christian preachers, we must be aware that Jesus Christ is our "frame of reference within which the OT witness is now to be appropriated."[18] This is obvious in the sample sermons throughout this book. Most sermons end by turning to Jesus as either the fulfillment or the final word. Still, preachers can also be sensitive to how the biblical text is interpreted and look wherever possible to not cause harm to others. When confronted, we should also be ready to listen and apologize for unintended harm.

This habit of Christians appropriating extends not just to the Hebrew Scriptures and applying them to Jesus, but the whole endeavor of preaching is to appropriate the Bible to our contemporary context. Preachers take these ancient stories from the Bible and bring them to a new group of people, presenting it as stories for them. This is quite a leap, though it is not always acknowledged. Capill describes the purpose of expository preaching as believing that through these stories, God is "speaking to them and is dealing with their lives."[19] Pasquarello suggests that the Bible itself uses "participatory language," encouraging hearers to "personally" appropriate and absorb

14. Stanton, *Woman's Bible*, 16.

15. Fuchs, *Feminist Theory*, 33.

16. Levine and Bretter, *Bible with and without Jesus*.

17. Levine, "When the Bible Becomes Weaponized," 197.

18. Moberly, "Preaching Christ from the Old Testament," 240.

19. Capill, *Heart Is the Target*, 45.

who God is and be changed, becoming more "disposed to godliness."[20] This is one way the Bible can be appropriated, though it is not the only way. Lake outlines how the Bible has been drawn on in many ways, impacting Australian culture. She says the Bible continues to be a text that is "variously interpreted," often appearing in startling ways, and is a "source of inspiration, power and practical wisdom" for a whole range of people.[21] The Bible is not contained just to Jews or Christians; many have appropriated and applied the Bible's stories to their situation. To complicate matters further, preachers also regularly draw on a range of other texts like books, movies, art, etc., to communicate. Homiletic texts will encourage preachers to "expand your horizons" by reading widely and developing a curiosity about the world, which then can be drawn on to illustrate points in their sermons.[22] The same questions I will ask about appropriation and the Bible can also be asked when borrowing stories and illustrations in sermons.

In many ways, drawing from a range of sources is a good thing. It enriches us, especially if we recognize we are part of a wider conversation. Appropriation is only seen to be problematic when there is a power imbalance causing harm. Preachers have not always thought about the power they have as speakers. Craddock writes how authority was seen as a positive until the 1960s, when all institutions, including religious institutions, began to be questioned. The role of the preacher was diminished.[23] Preachers have often been blind or uninterested in who occupies the pulpit. For a long time, it was seen to be natural and self-evident that white men should be the ones to preach. Indeed, there continues to be a debate in evangelical circles about whether God calls women to preach or whether it is forbidden. One of the underlying assumptions that men brought to preaching was that their experience was normative. McClure argues that modernist preachers believed and sought "common human experience" in their preaching through their illustrations and applications of the text.[24] Over the last few decades, the idea of a shared universal experience has been challenged by many, including feminist scholars. For example, Fuchs argues that the Bible itself, while seemingly addressing the common human experience, is androcentric, with women reduced in the biblical

20. Pasquarello, *Christian Preaching*, 74.

21. Lake, *Bible in Australia*, 369.

22. Kuruvilla, *Manual for Preaching*, 167–68.

23. Craddock, *As One Without Authority*, 14.

24. McClure, *Other-Wise Preaching*, 47.

narratives to "auxiliary roles," thus creating and fostering "a politics of male domination."[25] Christian women often grow accustomed to this perspective and learn to "read the text as men."[26] As discussed in previous chapters, such an appropriation of the Bible means many Christians uncritically accept and embrace the patriarchal portrayal of women and seek to maintain that perspective in our culture today. Shercliff takes a slightly different line to Fuchs. She does not believe the Bible itself is androcentric, but she does believe interpretation has been androcentric. Women's experiences and voices have been excluded for so long that they have become "an anomaly, unworthy of serious consideration."[27]

To counter this, preachers, especially those who make the decisions about who speaks, can commit to having a range of people preach in their local church. Martin Alcoff explains that this response comes from a growing awareness of each person's limitations.[28] Chapin Garner advises that when choosing what biblical character's perspective to speak from to create a first-person narrative sermon, it should be whatever character a preacher would like to choose.[29] I suspect we normally select the person we can identify with or the main character in the biblical text. It might not be a choice that men consider for long because they naturally gravitate to male characters, and men tend to be the main characters in the Bible. Men might also avoid choosing a female character because there is the danger that when those with more power use their voice to speak on behalf of another more marginalized group, it has often resulted in "increasing or reinforcing the oppression of that group."[30] This awareness of the wide range of subjectivities and marginality of some voices is one of the reasons we do not see men give first-person narratives from a woman's perspective. If a man tried to embrace a female character's perspective in preaching, I suspect it would seem so jarring because it would highlight how abnormal it is for women to appear in the biblical text. Men do not generally inhabit and appropriate women's perspectives because women are seen as more marginal. This does not mean it could never happen. Martin Alcoff offers some caveats, suggesting that appropriation is not black and white, and there might be times when it is

25. Fuchs, *Sexual Politics*, 11.
26. Fuchs, *Sexual Politics*, 16.
27. Shercliff, *Preaching Women*, chapter 5.
28. Alcoff, "Problem of Speaking for Others."
29. Garner, *Getting into Character*, 42.
30. Alcoff, "Problem of Speaking for Others," 98–99.

appropriate for someone with privilege to use their voice on behalf of others. To do so, critical awareness and humility are necessary.[31]

Appropriation and the Text

As we explored earlier, first-person narrative structures can be a powerful tool for female preachers because it allows them to respond to difficult texts by learning to reappropriate biblical stories. Christians do not just appropriate texts but also methods of interpretation. In Judges 19, for example, we read about a woman with little power. A woman has to make a choice when she is preparing to preach on such a text. She can either cover up the patriarchy by endorsing it or use her voice to challenge it. Feminists have appropriated this story to draw parallels to how our society can downplay women's voices and presence.[32] They understand that stories are powerful. The stories we tell shape our understanding of the world and our place in it. Scott outlines various ways a story can be retold, including what he names "restorying as recontextualising"—when the narrative structure remains the same, but there are differences with the storyteller deliberately disrupting the narrative in some way.[33] Fuchs has written about the potential for feminist midrash to be used as a promising way to respond to biblical stories. Fuchs defines midrash as the "creative and fictional reconstruction of biblical stories."[34] It can both reconstruct, offering more space for women's voices, and be a place to question the biblical narrative critically. The womanist scholar Gafney likewise draws on the Hebrew idea of "midrash" to retell the stories in the Hebrew Bible, reimagining and creating a new reading where "women and girls" are the focus and one goes about "intentionally including and centering on non-Israelite peoples and enslaved persons."[35] Evans, at a more popular level, influenced by Gafney, uses a whole range of genres to retell and play with the biblical text in order to help her and others continue to engage with

---

31. Alcoff, "Problem of Speaking for Others," 116.

32. Trible, *Texts of Terror*; Mullner, "Lethal Differences"; Jones-Warsaw, "Toward a Womanist Hermeneutic."

33. Scott, "Restorying," 11

34. Fuchs, "Jewish Feminist Approaches." It should be noted that the word "midrash" has multiple meanings. Neusner explains the various Jewish approaches to interpretation in his *What Is Midrash?*

35. Gafney, *Womanist Midrash*, 3.

the Bible and realize every person is being invited "to join in the Great Conversation between God and God's people."[36]

Judges 19 depicts a brutal assault. As in other stories from the book of Judges, we are introduced to a man, a Levite with a concubine who has become unfaithful to him, returning to her father's home. He comes to collect her, and then, as they are traveling back to his home, it grows dark, and they stop in Gibeah. An old man notices them and offers them hospitality in his house. That hospitality is interrupted by a "perverse lot" of men banging at the door, wanting to rape the Levite.[37] The old man offers his daughter, but when the daughter is rejected, the Levite pushes his concubine out instead. She is raped and collapses outside the door. The Levite picks her up and places her on his donkey in the morning. He cuts her body into pieces and calls on the tribes of Israel to avenge what has happened.

Many feminist scholars quickly point out from the very beginning of this story that the woman's voice and presence are downplayed. She is introduced in relationship to a man—commonly translated as a concubine, although this is actually misleading. She is a second wife.[38] Trible, who influentially commented on this story, notes the "dissonance" between this man and the woman.[39] One has power and prestige; the other is "virtually a slave."[40] This is a woman who will remain nameless for the entire story. That namelessness creates a distance, "making it harder to view her as a person in her own right."[41] But the woman does act—she leaves the man and returns to her father's house only to be pursued by the man who claims her for himself once more. Men and their desires are prioritized. Hospitality, it seems, only extends to men.[42] Exum suggests that part of this story's function is to punish the woman for her earlier exercise of autonomy; what is emphasized is that a woman's sexuality belongs to men.[43]

A woman can retell this story and highlight how this woman is both there and not there:

36. Evans, *Inspired*, 23.

37. Judg 16:22.

38. Exum, "Feminist Criticism," 83.

39. Trible, *Texts of Terror*, 66.

40. Trible, *Texts of Terror*, 66.

41. Exum, "Feminist Criticism," 82.

42. Trible, *Texts of Terror*, 75.

43. Exum, "Feminist Criticism," 83.

*The woman now follows behind the weary Levite, behind the slave,
as they go together to the old man's home and settle in for the night.
The men exchange stories and local news. The woman is silent.
Maybe you can hear her breathing, maybe you forgot she was there
until there is a knock on the door.*

One of the reasons why it is so powerful to hear a woman tell this story is because by hearing a woman's voice, we are bringing the woman in the story to the fore. This is what feminists argue for—the need to appropriate these ancient stories, expose the patriarchy embedded in them, and name it as a sin that needs to be resisted. For this reason, the fact that a woman is up the front preaching from this text already signals a significant change.

This appropriation is, on the whole, believed to be good and liberating. Although one of the critiques by Mullner, as noted earlier, is that some feminist interpretations run the risk of being antisemitic—we look back and condemn the past without examining our present.[44] Mullner suggests feminists can be too quick to identify with women from different cultural backgrounds and not acknowledge the real difference.[45] Jones-Warsaw also raises this concern. Writing as a Black woman, she tells of the pressure she feels to conform to white "standards of beauty and goodness;" this has real damaging consequences, with many Black women appropriating such standards leading to "our dismemberment and fragmentation."[46] Warsaw-Jones says she identifies with the concubine, right at the bottom of the social order, asked to separate her gender from her race to be accepted and heard by feminists.[47] These concerns are worth taking on board. Yet when a difficult story is retold and reworked to speak into our contemporary context, it can have fresh life. Now, this raises more questions—are we allowed to rework biblical stories? Because, in a sense, that might entail going against the grain—when a woman's perspective is the primary way we see this story, this is different from how the narrator creates and tells the same story. In many ways, we should expect a man to address this text. Yet, I believe this is one of the strengths of narrative. It is open-ended and invites people to wrestle and respond to the text.

44. Mullner, "Lethal Differences," 129.

45. Mullner, "Lethal Differences," 132. She proposes a reading that explores the differences as a key category to unpacking the story and seeing the multiple layers of harm that is caused not just to women but also to men.

46. Jones-Warsaw, "Toward a Womanist Hermeneutic," 183.

47. Jones-Warsaw, "Toward a Womanist Hermeneutic," 183.

Men should feel like they are not excluded from speaking about this text, though. It is important they do—they just might do it differently. Many of the similar themes could be highlighted if a male preacher focused on the Levite and exposed the way the Levite failed as a priest. Embry argues that this story critiques the state of the priesthood at the time of this writing, which was failing to care for the most vulnerable.[48] There is also a place for preachers to be taught to use their imagination and place themselves in the role of others in the text. Indeed, Brueggemann argues that one of the essential roles of a preacher is not just to imagine and empathize with others but first allow ourselves to "imagine the world as though YHWH . . . were a real character and an effective agent in the world."[49] Brueggemann describes a battle of images and ideas fighting for dominance, and preachers can have a role in contributing by reminding people of the new thing that God is doing and moving people towards wonder.[50] In many ways, this overlaps with the notion of reappropriating—we tell these stories each time asking God's Spirit to show us the new thing, the good news that needs to be heard and reframed, so it is good news for all people.

Appropriation and Listeners

A woman's voice sharing such a vulnerable story can remind those listening that there is still danger for women. Scrutiny and blame are still often placed on women. Exum draws out how the woman in the text is subtly blamed for leaving her husband and then draws parallels to how blame and responsibility for violence against women are placed on women.[51] Trible notes how often the church's response to this text has been silence, but to be silent is to fail to confront and name sin. Instead, preachers need to "take to heart this ancient story . . . confess its present reality."[52] I have preached from this story a few times now and have done so at a time when there have been women raising their voices and saying "enough is enough" regarding sexual violence and harassment.[53] A recent investigation by Baird reports that a large number of women seeking help from their pastors about domestic violence in

48. Embry, "Narrative Loss," 263.

49. Brueggemann, *Practice of Prophetic Imagination*, 2.

50. Brueggemann, *Practice of Prophetic Imagination*, 128.

51. Exum, "Feminist Criticism," 84.

52. Trible, *Texts of Terror*, 87.

53. Redwood, "Enough Is Enough."

their household were either not believed or they were told to "submit to their husbands."[54] A preacher, particularly a woman, can help the church join this conversation by speaking about the uncomfortable and heartbreaking reality of violence still happening against women today.

Conclusion

Narrative sermons are a powerful tool that preachers can use to communicate the good news of God. Yet, without crucial reflection, preachers can inadvertently cause damage or harm to those listening. As artists and storytellers in our wider culture grapple with the ethical obligations storytellers have and become increasingly sensitive to who is telling whose stories, this can invite preachers to consider whose stories we are telling. All preachers should approach the biblical stories we tell with humility and an awareness of who in our community is most vulnerable. Feminist scholars are leading the way in helping people to reappropriate potentially damaging stories and instead seek to bring healing and truth by taking familiar stories and retelling them. My sample sermon begins by framing the story I will tell from Judges with the stories we are hearing now and reminding our listeners why this story still needs to be told and retold:

> *Many stories we forget or never get told—stories of what happens behind closed doors. Sexual violence is still a reality for women today. And too often, they don't share it because they feel ashamed. Because they won't be heard. And the church just adds to that shame and silence by bringing God into it in really destructive ways . . . But maybe what we should be saying is: enough is enough. Surely, that is what God is saying.*

This is something preachers can easily incorporate into their preaching. It also reminds us of the imbalance in many of our churches about who we regularly hear. By thinking through appropriation, there is a challenge for all preachers to continue to find ways to give opportunities to a whole range of people to speak so we can hear the full range of what God is doing in the world.

---

54. Baird, "Domestic Violence." This has been confirmed in a more recent report commissioned by the Anglican Church of Australia, Powell and Pepper, "Family Violence Research," 19.

Sample Sermon[55]

There has been a roar of female voices this week and over the last few weeks speaking out, saying: enough is enough. Chanel Contos has released a sexual assault petition signed by hundreds of teenage girls recounting their experiences in high school. It is confronting reading.[56] Brittney Higgins has spoken out about what allegedly happened to her in Parliament House.[57] Grace Tame, the Australian of the Year, keeps speaking out this week in Hobart, saying, "Evil thrives in silence, it's time to make some noise."[58] It is overwhelming, heartbreaking, and uncomfortable to hear these women speak about sexual violence. These are the voices erupting in our public square, voices and stories that some might be shocked to hear unless you have heard such voices speak before, perhaps in more private conversations. When I was a teenager, a friend of mine the same age disclosed to me a story of sexual abuse in her family just as we were sitting together at school eating lunch. I don't think I fully grasped what she was telling me, but I saw she was alone, and there was nobody else she thought she could turn to. I know of a woman who is a single mother. She lives with her parents after they rescued her from a husband who controlled how much money she could spend, whose only words were words that insulted, cut her, and made her small. I have friends who have talked to me about sexual harassment in the workplace. Women's voices can too often be absent from the public square and the church, missing. For much of history, women's voices have been silenced. Even I have to admit it. Their voices can be absent, missing, or reduced in our Bibles.

I hear the roar of women saying enough is enough. Then, I opened up to Judges 19. One of the worst stories for women in the Bible. It is overwhelming, heartbreaking, and uncomfortable. It is not even the first story we have heard in the book of Judges that deals with gendered violence. This is an entrenched pattern that comes up again and again, signaling this is not a once-off, isolated event but very much a part of the culture and structures of the day, just like in Australia, where one in five women have experienced sexual violence. On average, one woman a week is murdered by her current or former partner. At work, almost one in two women have experienced

---

55. A recording of this sermon can be found at Redwood, "Enough Is Enough."

56. Kozaki and Xiao, "Sydney Private School Students' Allegations."

57. Maiden, "Young Staffer Brittany Higgins."

58. Tame, "Culture of Silence."

sexual harassment in their lifetime.[59] These statistics, the women we are hearing in our public sphere, are signaling this is not a once-off, isolated incident but very much still part of our culture and structures, so I have to keep talking about this. I want to recognize that you might already be feeling overwhelmed, heartbroken, or uncomfortable. Especially if you have been abused. So, let's make sure we are taking care of one another and the responses we might have today. If you need to step out this morning, please do. I have the number on the screen if what we are talking about today raises things for you, and you need someone who you can talk to. I tell this story in Judges 19 in order to speak up and bring to light what can too often be hidden behind closed doors. And as I tell this story, I want you to pay attention: listen to who speaks and who doesn't speak. Whose eyes do we see this story from? Who acts and who doesn't act?

There was an old man coming home from work. In the twilight, he saw something, he looked, he saw: a man, a Levite, standing in the public square looking a little lost. Nobody had taken him in, nobody had provided hospitality. The old man was not from the tribe of Benjamin like the others in the town; he was from Ephraim, but still, Benjamin and Ephraim were all part of Israel, and he knew that the Israelites were meant to always offer hospitality to the stranger, particularly a Levite since they had received no land. It was part of their law, part of their worship to Yahweh. But nobody in this town had offered this Levite help. The old man asked the Levite, where are you going? Where have you come from? And the Levite answered: "We're coming from Bethlehem to the remote country . . ."

Oh, yes, only then did the old man notice the other people with the traveler in the shadows. A woman. And a young man, a slave perhaps. A glimpse, but then the old man's attention returned to the Levite. The Levite stressed how he had everything he needed: straw and fodder for the donkeys, bread, and wine. They just needed a place to sleep. The old man knew that the world was not so safe, especially once night fell, so he offered the Levite hospitality: welcome; come into my home, it is late, come, eat and drink with me.

The woman standing with the Levite hears that word: *home*. The word should conjure up warmth, security, love, and perhaps, a safe space from an often chaotic world, like the word *family*. Family is meant to connect you to others, bring order. Family protects, gives love. But these words have lost their meaning for the woman, if she ever even knew them. Sometimes,

59. Topsfield, "Half of All Australian Women Sexually Harassed."

a family does not protect. It just takes. They allow the door to be open, and chaos comes in. The woman standing there behind the men thinks about how she was taken, taken by this Levite, becoming his second wife. Some call her his concubine. Some call her unfaithful, a harlot because she left him. She didn't want to be with him, so she went back to her father's home, trying to find some protection there. But her father welcomed this man into his house and opened the door. They ate and drank together. They ate and drank for five days before her husband decided he needed to act. It was time to go, and she needed to follow him. They left too late; the slave suggested stopping in at Jebus for the night, but her husband rejected the idea, not wanting to associate himself with foreigners. They pushed on to this town, the town of Gibeah.

The woman now follows behind the weary Levite, behind the slave, as they go together to the old man's home and settle in for the night. The men exchange stories and local news. The woman is silent. Maybe you can hear her breathing. Maybe you forgot she was there until there is a knock on the door. Knock is perhaps too polite a word. It is more a thumping that grows louder and louder, a hammering of bodies slamming into the door calling for the Levite to be brought outside: "Open the door, open the door, so we can know you."

Chaos calls. A mob of men want to take, shame, destroy. Want to have some fun with this stranger? The man is suddenly not safe. How odd to be in such a position. The old man begs them to spare the Levite, but it makes no difference. He even offers them to take my daughter and take the woman with him. And when that is not enough, her man, her husband, opens the door and thrusts her outside. She is given so he might be spared, safe. Let the chaos devour her.

And the woman we barely know, the woman with no name, so quiet you might have missed her, is abused all night. Raped. And nobody comes to save her. They leave her there. She drifts out of her own body, detached, her body broken. There are tears on her face, but she can't feel them anymore. Morning comes, light spills over the threshold, the men let her go, and she stumbles and falls down at the front of the door.

Her husband opens the door when it is silent, when the day brings safety, and the morning makes everything look so different that it's almost like the night before was a bad dream, so he resumes his journey, stepping over the woman at the door. Oh yes, her. Impatient, he commands her, "Get up; let us be going." Silly woman, lying on the ground like that. But there is no response. Finally, she is fully silent. So he has to heave her up and carry her to his home. There, he takes out a knife and carves out her body into twelve pieces to the tribes of Israel. Now wanting justice or vengeance or something, he rouses the tribes, and they come, and there is more killing and death, and the woman whose name we don't know is lost amid it all.

This is not a nice story to tell. Perhaps you have never heard it before, perhaps it is better to keep it in the background. To stay quiet. This is not a nice story to tell to middle-class suburbia, where we think things are different now. Everyone is safe here, right? Safe in our homes and families, safe on the streets at night. God will protect. God is with us. Yet God does not appear in this story in Judges 19. Here is a truth we learn or know deep down: terrible things happen, and we are not always spared from them. Many injustices go uncorrected. Many stories we forget or never get told. Stories of what happens behind closed doors. Sexual violence is still a reality for women today. And too often, they don't share it because they feel ashamed. Because they won't be heard. And the church just adds to that shame and silence by bringing God into it in really destructive ways. A few years ago, Julia Baird and Hayley Gleeson reported how many women are told to be silent when they tell their stories to their pastor.[60] If it happens in their home and they are married, they are told to stay and submit. Or just pray about it. Or examine themselves for sin. There but for the grace of God, we all go.

But maybe what we should be saying is: enough is enough. Surely, that is what God is saying. Enough is enough. Our God is a God who hears every voice, particularly those voices that are silenced. We might want to forget or pretend like bad things don't happen. We might be tempted not to be bothered to ask the woman in Judges 19: what was your name? But we have this terrible story in the book of Judges, and it exposes us because if you read the biblical text and ask whose eyes we see the story from, it's not this second wife, this woman. The focus is on the men, those with more power. Whose voices do we hear in Judges 19? Men's. The woman is barely there in the text. I have emphasized her today, but she is almost invisible until she is pushed outside, and too often, that is still the case. Who gets to act in Judges 19? The men decide to throw her out. There is a serious power imbalance at work here, and we need to say: Enough is enough. Something needs to change.

60. Baird, "Domestic Violence."

The good news is that this story is not meant to be the final word. It is unfinished. It shows a world where God's reign is not recognized. A society is disintegrating. And although her voice seems silent, her silence is a roar. The good news is this: God became one of us, Jesus, and Jesus is unlike so many other men. Jesus looked at the people others ignored; he listened to their voices, and then he spoke and acted by welcoming them, eating and drinking with the sinners and the so-called prostitutes, healing and inviting people to make their home with God. Here is a person who loves. Who surrenders his power. Jesus shows grace even though he knows the world is not safe. But this is who God is.

His voice disturbs those in power. So, they act. They come in the middle of the night once more, another mob thumping through a garden. Chaos calls. They want to take, shame, destroy Jesus. And he lets them. He doesn't let someone else be the sacrifice. He doesn't let his friends take up arms and fight. He lets himself be arrested and endures a mock trial. He gives himself so that others might be spared. And as we, human beings, do what we so often do: mutilate and destroy, crucify an innocent person, God lets the chaos devour. Saying: Enough is enough.

At the cross, injustice and sin are nailed there. Chaos is dealt with. The power balance is upended. All those things that happen behind closed doors that shouldn't, all those people whose blood has soaked the ground that cried out to God with their last breath, where are you? They are answered here. Jesus dies with them and for them, the victims and the perpetrators. And then, three days later, God raises Jesus from the dead, breathing new life into Jesus' lungs. God can lift us up into new possibilities. A new kingdom is coming.

For those who have hurt or are deeply hurt, God knows, and God acts and will act, bringing justice and hope. Don't be afraid to speak. We need to hear your voices. And for all of us, don't be afraid to listen. The Baptist Association has been training pastors and churches in how to deal with domestic violence, first running a campaign about four years ago.[61] The church declares that Jesus is our ruler, and we follow him. To follow him means we should be ready and willing to join our voices with those women and say enough is enough. This is not what God intended for us. There is a better way. We will work towards being a community that sees and hears all people. We will work especially to hear the vulnerable. We will work towards creating a culture where people feel safe and can flourish.

61. "Safer Spaces Toolkit."

At a very practical level, what might this look like? Well, this is from the Baptist Association's page on this, and it doesn't cover everything, but it is a start. If someone shares their story with you:

1. Listen to the person disclosing the violence. Believe her/him. Ensure that abuse cannot be accepted in any circumstances. Do not blame the victim or ask what they have done to contribute to the violence.

2. Be sure to empower the victim. Do not make decisions for her/him. Ask how she/he wants you to help. Affirm they are the person best placed to map a path forward. Respect her/his right to make decisions.

3. It is important to remember: If there is imminent risk of harm, call 000.

4. Keep offering support.

   1800 RESPECT (1800 737 732)

   NSW DV hotline (1800 656 463)

   Mensline NSW (1300 789 978)[62]

Discussion Questions

Have you ever seen a man preach a first-person narrative as a female character? How did you respond?

Do preachers need to consider how we use wider cultural stories (especially if they are not our stories)?

How important is it to you as a preacher to engage with Jewish interpreters when working in the Old Testament?

Exercise

Read a novel by someone who is not a Christian who draws on the Bible or listen to someone from another religion speak on the Bible. Try to incorporate their insights into your sermon.

---

62. "Safer Spaces Toolkit."

7

The Process

I WORK IN A small church on the Northern Beaches in Sydney, New South Wales. Most weeks, we gather on Sundays. People listen to me, a female preacher, talking to a mixed congregation.[1] As the pastor, I invite people to preach at our church. I invite women and men to speak. I researched feminist scholarship and the book of Judges because I was looking for role models I could learn from. I wanted to examine my interpretative choices when I approached the Bible and prepared my sermons. I decided to do this by learning from different people whose voices and perspectives would stretch and question my interpretative choices. I wanted to grow as a preacher, and I believed this would be beneficial not just for me but also for other preachers.

Before dialoguing with others, I needed to delve into and identify my presuppositions. Every preacher needs to do this. In chapter 1, I defined what I meant by the terms "evangelical" and "egalitarian." One of the central beliefs for evangelical preachers is that the Bible is the word of God, bringing the good news about how we can come to know God through Jesus Christ. This is why preaching is so important. Evangelicals trust this ancient work still has something to say to our contemporary context. Evangelicals agree on this point but disagree on their understanding of what the Bible says, for example, about gender. Egalitarians understand the Scriptures to

1. For those who are unsure what "mixed congregation" means, it is a congregation that comprises both males and females (LGBTQI+ people are not normally considered under this label, but I think they need to be).

128

celebrate people, both females and males, as created in the image of God. Women and men are equal ontologically and functionally. Complementarians would also understand the Scriptures to celebrate people, both males and females, as created in the image of God. Then, they would argue that men and women have different roles. Males are to lead, and females are to submit, particularly in marriage and church leadership. It is essential to recognize this difference among evangelicals. An egalitarian might think a feminist perspective can positively contribute to evangelical preaching. A complementarian is more likely to view feminism as a challenge. First and foremost, I want to encourage other egalitarian preachers. However, later in this chapter, I also want to address complementarians and express my hope for how this book could benefit them.

Our presuppositions as preachers shape how we interpret the biblical text. There is a wide-ranging hermeneutical discussion about the task of interpretation and the relationship between the reader, author, and text. I entered this conversation by using Gadamer as a guide. Gadamer argues that presuppositions are unavoidable and essential. We need to recognize them and the tradition(s) we are working in. Then, we approach the text. Gadamer uses the metaphor of dialogue to describe how meaning is formed: we listen to the text and impact the text in a sense. Through this encounter, a new understanding emerges. Evangelicals would find some of Gadamer's ideas uncomfortable because of our high regard for Scripture. One of the tensions is who has more power in this scenario: the reader or the text (presuming the text also has an author connected to it). Evangelicals want to give priority to the text. In relation to this, Vanhoozer argues that holding a critical realist position is entirely valid. A critical realist believes you can know what the author meant to communicate through the text, although you also recognize our knowledge is incomplete. There are things we will not know or we will distort. One way to help us identify potential distortions is to listen to people with different presuppositions and see what they notice in the text. This is one of the reasons I have chosen to engage with feminist scholars. So, what have I learned as I have preached from the book of Judges focusing on the women and their stories? I will reflect on what I have learned one last time through these three angles: the preacher, the listener, and the text.

The Preacher

The best way for me to begin to answer this question is to talk about my experience dialoguing with non-evangelical feminist scholars. It has profoundly shaped me. In the first chapter, I stated that one of the motivations for pursuing this research was to think about how my gender shaped my preaching and interpretation of Scripture. I began as an egalitarian. But I wanted to downplay my gender. I did not want people to notice that I was a woman! I hated feeling like I stood out because of that fact. Feminist scholarship can contribute to helping evangelical female preachers acknowledge and explore how gender shapes us. By listening to feminists, I have become more comfortable leaning into and embracing my gender, especially regarding the stories that feature women in the Bible. I have realized I can say things about women's stories in the book of Judges that men cannot say with the same effect.

I have come to recognize that I need to expand my emotional range. Feminist scholars were more likely than evangelical scholars to identify the uncomfortable parts of the biblical story and respond with anger and lament. As an evangelical woman, I have avoided expressing anger in my sermons. I did not want to be perceived as a "shrill woman." Yet, I believe churches need to equip and help women and men express their anger healthily. There is a growing conversation happening in our contemporary context regarding gender, and many emotions, including anger, are expressed. Evangelicals could find ways to join this conversation by drawing from some of the complicated stories we find ourselves wrestling with in the Bible, like the stories in the book of Judges, and bring them into our context.

Feminist scholarship challenges preachers by exposing the ways patriarchal ideology can impact us. Reading feminist scholars has challenged me to acknowledge that women are absent in much of our Scriptures. The fact that I still feel we need to talk about women reminds me that women do not often appear in the Bible. When they are present, Fuchs rightly raises concerns—asking what ideological agenda they are promoting. This has forced me to ask similar questions of myself. Even though I identified as an egalitarian, I have realized how deep patriarchal ideology runs in me.

In 2017, I changed roles, becoming the senior pastor at Seaforth Baptist. My preaching increased in frequency. Those first six months were challenging. I was very uncomfortable being the primary preacher. My theology was egalitarian, but deep down, the influences of complementarianism remained strong in me. I was worried that people would get bored listening to me! I was worried that I did not command the same authority as a male preacher. I started rushing out to bring in male guest preachers. I had to rediscover my voice, and reading feminist scholars helped. They allowed me to see beyond myself and recognize the structures and systems that deliberately limit women. For instance, I have become uncomfortable with describing God using masculine pronouns. I think this subtly reinforces the idea that men are the natural leaders and speakers in the church. I also have become increasingly frustrated when I look at my denomination's theological college and senior leadership: all I see are men. Again, the implicit message reinforced is that men are likely to be promoted and recognized as leaders. Some female leadership is tolerated, but there is a limit. As an evangelical preacher, it is very easy for me to apply and promote patriarchal ideology.

So, I have changed as a preacher. The word *egalitarian* does not seem strong enough anymore. The temptation as an evangelical is to smooth away the difficult parts of the Bible. Evangelicals want to see the best in the Scriptures and downplay the complex parts. In the past, I was sometimes careful when people asked me what I was researching: when I thought someone might be complementarian, I didn't mention the word *feminist*. Egalitarianism feels like a softer word than feminism, so I think I have used it to avoid offending people and to be accepted by the evangelical church.[2] It can be hard for egalitarian evangelicals to recognize the systems they are working in. As discussed in chapter 4, I have wanted to be a good evangelical woman by not causing a fuss. Yet the reality is that many evangelicals claim to be egalitarian, but their practices do not always match their beliefs.[3] I realize I need to embrace "feminism" more and say I am not just an evangelical egalitarian preacher—I want to be an evangelical feminist preacher. Feminist scholars often approach the text warily and ready to resist. I tend to come to the biblical text prepared to trust and embrace. However, feminist scholars challenged me to consider when I might need to resist. I might be parting from the majority of evangelical preachers, but after interacting with non-evangelical feminist scholars, I have been persuaded that the biblical text at

2. While writing this book this was confirmed when I read that the term "egalitarian" was coined to distinguish itself from secular feminism or more progressive Christian feminism; the word is part of "the more conservative part" of evangelicalism. See Lee-Barnewall, *Neither Complementarian nor Egalitarian*, Introduction.

3. This has been recently researched by Lauve-Moon, who examines conscious and unconscious hiring practices of egalitarian churches seeking to call pastors. See Lauve-Moon, "Preacher Woman."

times depicts damaging ideologies, even promotes (unintentionally or not) damaging ideologies. This means that sometimes the application called for is resistance to damaging ideology both in the biblical text and in our contemporary context. A reparative reading strategy could be a way forward for evangelicals. This approach seeks to listen, engage with resistant readings, and look for signs of redemption and hope in the text.

I am trying to be a preacher and an academic. I am active in both spaces, although my focus remains on the local church. I have a growing passion for equipping preachers, particularly egalitarian female preachers. I want to encourage women like I was encouraged but with a difference. I was inspired primarily by men. As a woman, I can offer other women what I did not have. I have come to recognize that I function as a role model. Becoming more active in collaborations and networks focused on building up female preachers is exciting. I believe being part of such a network can be one way people can support and encourage female preachers.

I hope this book also contributes to building up male egalitarian evangelical preachers. I recognize I have focused primarily on being a female egalitarian preacher. I wanted to show how the preacher's identity drives so much of the interpretation and preaching process—our gender matters. Yet, at the same time, I believe as we dialogue with others and, even better, form relationships with people who are different from us, we can incorporate their contributions to our reading of Scripture. This book might feel like it has nothing worthwhile to say to male egalitarian preachers, but that is not the case. Feminist scholarship challenges male preachers to grapple with how their gender shapes their reading of the text. Nobody is neutral. Male preachers, too, have blind spots and will miss things in the biblical text. This is why male preachers need to diversify who they listen to and read. Dialoguing with feminist scholarship is one avenue worth exploring. Many of the insights I have discovered, like listening to and inhabiting marginal characters in the text, could be applied by male preachers.

Every now and then, I get invited to panels addressing the lack of female leadership in the evangelical church. Those panels are often comprised of women—sharing their experiences. There is a general desire by some to see more female leaders and preachers. But having a general desire is not enough. Even though male egalitarian preachers might think they support female leadership in the church, this needs to be coupled with action. Male egalitarian preachers need to be reading theological books written by women, have female preachers they look to as role models, and intentionally create opportunities for women to preach and join the pastoral team. I would love to see more evangelical men taking serious steps in this direction.

Token women are not enough. One of the reasons feminist scholars are drawn to the book of Judges is that it features women. It is one of the reasons why I chose it. Women rarely feature in (or at the center of) biblical narratives, and I got used to their rarity. So, we have to single them out and pay extra attention to how the biblical texts featuring women should be applied. But going forward, I do not want to treat women as rare tokens. I do not want to be in the same situation as the book of Judges! I want us to have moved forward.[4] For that to happen, feminist scholarship cannot just be scholarship that is confined to women or the academy. This is one of the advantages of preaching. Preaching allows feminist scholarship to have a broader audience. It will enable the average member of a church to be exposed to and challenged on these issues. Male egalitarian preachers can play a role here.

It is harder to answer how this book might inform complementarian preachers. I hope that perhaps when someone hears one of these sermons or something like it, they might hear God and be open to entering into a dialogue with someone with very different presuppositions. At the very least, an evangelical preacher might be willing to learn from people who are different from them—I think that is an important place to start. When we do so, we should be prepared to be changed. Interacting with the biblical text changes us, and interacting with others can change us too. But this need not make us afraid. Feminist scholarship has much to contribute to and challenge evangelical theology and homiletics, and this dialogue needs to continue to unsettle and enlighten us.

Listeners

Feminism is part of the contemporary context. It's easy to forget our context until you encounter another context. The book of Judges can seem like a foreign and ancient book with little to say to contemporary listeners. Nonetheless, feminist scholars helped me connect to the modern discussion on gender. Over the last few years, the conversation around gender has grown in our wider culture. I have addressed some of the live issues that have come up

4. I am drawn to Webb's idea of a redemptive-movement hermeneutic. See Webb, *Slaves, Women and Homosexuals.*

in previous chapters, including domestic violence, workplace harassment, and the #MeToo movement. The fact that this conversation is alive reinforces the need for evangelical preachers to engage with feminist scholars so that they may know their listeners more. Feminism can call congregations to the margins and highlight people we can easily overlook.

In 2021, I brought my research into the life of an actual congregation. We worked through the whole book of Judges for twelve Sundays, entering the season of Lent about halfway through the series. Immediately, I was confronted by listeners responding. Some were outraged and distressed that we spent so much time in such a violent book. I needed to visit a family's home and listen to their concerns. Others were excited and provoked and wanted to catch up and chat further. Now, in some ways, this can be a preacher's dream. We long to see people wanting to engage. It was surprising to see Judges create such a stir. I quickly realized that what I was asking of this church was huge: to spend so long in such a dark book is not easy. This could be why I cannot recall hearing the whole of the book of Judges preached before. It is a book you might briefly visit, particularly if you are involved in kids' ministry. You can jump into some of the famous stories like Samson and Delilah. Still, nobody wants to linger long—and here I was calling on these listeners to give twelve Sundays to this book!

I was also reminded how much context shapes the sermon. This is something feminist scholarship contributes to as well. Bal and Fuchs are conscious of their social location. There were subtle changes I had to make when bringing the sermons to a church. I initially wrote many of these sermons for my thesis and then delivered them to a congregation. The sermon on Judges 4–5 with multiple voices was quite emotional to preach in person. I do not think I fully appreciated how difficult it would be to preach such a sermon. First, I gave plenty of notice, warning people that this might be difficult to hear and might trigger trauma. This turned out to be accurate, as one listener did come up to me afterward to talk about the sexual abuse she had experienced. Second, it took an emotional toll on me as I tried to inhabit Jael. It was a heavy place to sit in. There was also an emotional toll on the congregation. After the sermon, we played some reflective music and had time to respond, but everyone was still processing, so people sat there in silence even after the service had concluded. It hit a nerve with some of the people listening. People identified with Jael's need for bloody justice and then felt confused and challenged as they heard Sisera's mother missing her son. One of the applications I did not fully anticipate was people questioning some of our notions around justice and punishment. Seeing and hearing different perspectives opened people's eyes to how what seems like justice for one person might not be experienced that way by another person. Feminist scholarship challenges people to listen to voices they are not used to hearing.

When preaching on Jephthah's daughter, I honestly wasn't sure how my sermon bringing feminism and postcolonialism together would be received. In the middle of the congregation was a couple I thought were complementarian. I wondered if they would feel uncomfortable with my strong tone. Yet the most surprising thing happened when I said, "It's not always a good thing to be a good girl"—the wife spontaneously started clapping! It turned out she had just embarked on reading more feminist literature. Many people commented afterward that they had never seen me so passionate and wanted to see it more! A few weeks later, I preached on the Levite's concubine. Given the context I was speaking in, I think this sermon also really connected. That week our news had been filled with sexual harassment and rape allegations in Federal Parliament.[5] These sermons were speaking into the cultural moment.

In 2023, I returned to the book of Judges and created two more sermons for this book around Achsah and Delilah. My first-person narrative sermon on Achsah was given to a new congregation. I was a guest preacher and had been invited to come and share on a woman from the Scriptures. I was speaking in an affirming church in the city of Sydney. I had formed this sermon without this particular congregation in mind, but it felt like I had prepared it for them. I was conscious that the theme of forgetting and invisibility presses heavily on many LGBTQI+ people. My sermon on Delilah has yet to be delivered to a real congregation.

After delivering these sermons to real people, I can see just how powerful feminist scholarship can be for evangelical preachers. To be honest, most weeks, a preacher does not get a lot of feedback from listeners (unless looking bored counts!), but the sermons from the book of Judges provoked a range of reactions. I could see people were paying attention in a way that does not always happen. There is a hunger from listeners for sermons that speak into their experiences and challenge them. Feminist scholarship can help evangelical preachers do exactly this because non-evangelical feminist scholars are interested in the contemporary context. They read and sometimes resist the biblical text because

5. Maiden, "Young Staffer."

they are concerned with its impact on women and men today. This focus on application is something evangelical preachers should care about, but application is often weak. Evangelical preachers have rigorous training in understanding the Bible in its original context but less training when it comes to knowing our context. Dialoguing with various people can help expand an evangelical's understanding of the wider world.

The Biblical Text

An evangelical proclaims and trusts in the good news of Jesus Christ as described for us in the Bible. At least, that is what an evangelical is meant to be at its most stripped-down definition. The word *evangelical* has become associated with certain political leanings and/or a more conservative approach to contemporary moral and ethical issues.[6] Before I started listening to feminist scholars, my general approach when preaching was to look at one or two evangelical commentaries. These commentaries usually confirmed what I was already discovering in my reading. Shared presuppositions make it easier. I can see how helpful they could be if you need quick clarity as a busy preacher. I appreciated their attention to detail as they worked verse by verse through the text. This is something I think feminist scholars can learn from evangelicals. The authors tried their best to be neutral, although their theological convictions were clear. I was only jolted by their perspectives when the complementarians read the text in a way I would not. But these commentaries rarely ever strayed into our contemporary context. I needed to do the work of application alone, and so I did. Immersing myself in feminist scholarship has changed the way I approach the Bible.

While I would still affirm that God inspires the Bible, the Bible has become less black and white. It does not feel like a static text anymore. Gushee writes as someone from an evangelical background who has shifted beyond evangelicalism.[7] He critiques evangelicals when they fall into a "near idolatry of the Bible."[8] He challenges us to a "heighten[ed] realism about the fact that the Bible is always an interpreted text and that we flawed, limited,

---

6. Du Mez traces this development in the US. Australia, while a different place, is certainly influenced by US evangelicalism. See Du Mez, *Jesus and John Wayne.*

7. In this transition Gushee has not landed on an exact definition of where he now stands except to speak of a post-evangelical position.

8. Gushee, *After Evangelicalism*, 30.

self-interested people are the interpreters."[9] Reading the Bible now feels more dynamic; I am conversing with God's people as they wrestle with how God is working in their time and place. This helps explain how women like Deborah can be celebrated and other women forgotten, like Jephthah's daughter. It seems to me there is a myriad of voices in the Bible presenting different sides of an issue. Bal touched on this when she raised the idea that Judges 5 could have derived from a female oral tradition. There is also a myriad of voices speaking about what the Bible means. I am one voice connected to both the Bible and the church. An evangelical preacher must remember that we interpret and speak as part of a broader conversation that extends from the past to the present. It is a "communal process."[10] Perhaps one of the lasting impacts of this research for me is the recognition that exegesis and application are deeply linked and cannot be neatly divided as evangelicals tend to claim and operate. As I have written these sermons and reflected on the application process, I have realized that the lines between interpretation and application are not fixed. The feminist scholars I examined were much more aware of their context and asked different questions of the biblical text as a result. There was a playfulness in their approach I have learned to embrace. I have become comfortable and aware of my social location, shaping how I preach the Bible in a contemporary context.

I have embraced my imagination a lot more. I have become fascinated by what Fuchs mentions regarding the Jewish midrash. Gushee writes that the Jewish tradition respects the Scriptures by "debating it and its interpreters."[11] Evangelical preachers could investigate and explore the Jewish tradition further. Feminism continues to expand with new readings happening from a womanist perspective. There is also a broader discussion on gender and sexuality. One of the images that represents how I see preachers is that of a storyteller. This has undoubtedly affected the sample sermons, as does the fact that the biblical texts I was seeking to preach from are narrative (with the exception of the song in Judges 5). These genres shaped my approach. All of the sermons, to one degree or another, are story-based and draw on creativity. Bal and Fuchs's unexpected contributions have been to expand whose stories I am telling in the Bible and how I tell them.

9. Gushee, *After Evangelicalism*, 36.

10. Gushee, *After Evangelicalism*, 36–37.

11. Gushee, *After Evangelicalism*, 39.

Bal's counter-coherence approach contributed to me giving my first-person narrative sermon in 2018. I had played a bit with narrative sermons before, telling third-person narratives featuring women like Esther and the women who discovered Jesus' empty tomb. But I had never tried a first-person narrative sermon until I was researching the book of Judges. I started with Hagar.[12] Learning from Bal, I listened to a minor character in the Genesis story and amplified her voice. It was one of the most powerful sermons I had ever given. Since then, I have given a range of first-person sermons, amplifying Rachel's voice, the woman caught in adultery and brought to Jesus, the disciples walking on the road to Emmaus, and the Levite's concubine in Judges 19.[13] This has become a standard tool I now use in preaching. First-person narrative sermons are not a new idea for preachers, but Bal's theory of counter-coherence helps clarify and provide a deeper theological framework for why this type of sermon can be effective. People long for their stories to be heard and know they have value in God's story. Yet, women's voices are often muted in the Bible. Bal's approach encourages people to challenge themselves by listening to the dominant and minor narrative beats. In doing so, we can amplify and celebrate a range of voices. This is a sermon structure that any evangelical preacher could pick up and use.

Feminist scholars tend to skip around not in chronological order but where they see connections. For instance, Fuchs's starting point for Judges 11 was to ask questions about the formation of the nation of Israel and how that impacted women. This is how application happens—when we have questions outside the original text. As we look, we start to see lines of connection or disconnection. These feminist scholars asked different questions of the text and, therefore, saw things I missed. Feminist scholarship can contribute to evangelical preaching because of the questions it raises. I had never interacted with postcolonial readings before, yet when I did, I saw and asked questions about the text I had not asked before. This is a commitment I want to take with me—to continue this habit of dialoguing with different people, particularly those on the margins.

12. Redwood, "God Who Sees."

13. Redwood and Mawson, "Leah and Rachel"; Redwood, "Storytelling"; "Road to Emmaus"; "Enough Is Enough."

Conclusion

Throughout this book, I have sought to model the value of dialogue. Exegesis and application are in a dialogue together. A preacher enters a dialogue with the biblical text and their congregation. Individuals and communities are invited into a conversation with God. I believe the dialogical model is compelling in our contemporary context. Application inhabits the intersection between a preacher, the biblical text, and the listeners. Evangelical preachers need to recognize their presuppositions. We come to the Bible and enter an ongoing conversation with God and God's people. We can bring our whole selves to this task. We can bring our imaginations, our social locations, our gender, our theological tradition, our reason, and the conversations that are happening around us. Then, to apply and communicate the gospel of Jesus, we need to be committed to learning from others. Evangelical preachers should be willing to listen to people with different presuppositions, particularly marginal people, and ask how they read the text. Such a dialogue can help us dig deeper into the text and ask questions we have never considered. Feminist scholarship does precisely this: the church is missing a valuable resource when it stays in the academy. Feminist scholarship can contribute to and challenge evangelical preachers by highlighting the voices and the absence of female voices in the Bible, particularly the book of Judges. Feminist scholars encourage us to bring female voices to people's attention. I invite you to listen.

> *I hear the Holy Spirit speaking,*
> *Through these non-evangelical feminist scholars.*
> *For the sake of the evangelical church, I listen.*
> *I hear God calling me to preach*
> *And join my voice singing and lamenting.*
> *For the sake of the evangelical church, I listen.*
> *Do not forget Achsah.*
> *Remember and tell her story.*
> *Evangelicals, will you listen?*
> *I hear Jael—saying, "no more!"*
> *I hear Sisera's mother anxious for her son.*
> *Evangelicals, will you listen?*
> *I tell the story of Jephthah's daughter,*
> *So that her story will not be possible in the future.*
> *Evangelicals, will you listen?*

Sometimes, it will mean I can't be a good girl.
I might need to resist. But if I resist, it is out of love.
For the sake of the evangelical church, will you listen?
Delilah, the wrong woman, the bad woman,
What do you feel about your story?
Can we sit with uncomfortable emotions?
Evangelicals, will you listen?
Even in the silence of the unnamed concubine,
For the women whose voices we still don't get to hear.
I will try to pay attention and amplify you.
For the sake of the evangelical church, will you listen?

Bibliography

Achtemeier, Elizabeth. "The Canon as the Voice of the Living God." In *Reclaiming the Bible for the Church*, edited by Carl E. Braaten et al., 119–30. Edinburgh: T. & T. Clark, 1995.

Adam, Peter. "Australia—Whose Land? A Call for Recompense." John Saunders Lecture. Sydney: Morling College, 2009.

Alatrash, Ghada. "When a Mother Loses Her Sons to a Merciless War." *The Globe and Mail*, May 10, 2019. https://www.theglobeandmail.com/opinion/article-when-a-mother-loses-her-sons-to-a-merciless-war/.

Alcoff, Linda Martin. "The Problem of Speaking for Others." In *Who Can Speak?: Authority and Critical Identity*, edited by Judith Roof et al., 97–119. Urbana: University of Illinois Press, 1995.

Allam, Lorena, et al. "The 474 Deaths Inside: Tragic Toll of Indigenous Deaths in Custody Revealed." *Guardian Australia*, April 9, 2021. https://www.theguardian.com/australia-news/2021/apr/09/the-474-deaths-inside-rising-number-of-indigenous-deaths-in-custody-revealed.

Allen, Ronald J. *Preaching and the Other: Studies of Postmodern Insights*. St. Louis: Chalice, 2009.

———. "Theology Undergirding Narrative Preaching." In *What's the Shape of Narrative Preaching?*, edited by Mike Graves et al., 27–40. St. Louis: Chalice, 2008.

Alston, Wallace M., and Cynthia A. Jarvis. *The Power to Comprehend with All the Saints: The Formation and Practice of a Pastor-Theologian*. Grand Rapids: Eerdmans, 2009.

Alter, Robert. *The Art of Biblical Poetry*. New York: Basic, 1985.

Amador, J. D. H. "Feminist Biblical Hermeneutics: A Failure of Theoretical Nerve." *Journal of the American Academy of Religion* 66 (Spring 1998) 39–57.

Arthur, Sarah. *The God-Hungry Imagination: The Art of Storytelling for Postmodern Youth Ministry*. Nashville: Upper Room, 2007.

Arthurs, Jeffrey D. "The Fundamentals of Sermon Application (Part 2)." In *Interpretation and Application*, edited by Jeffrey D. Arthurs and Craig Brian Larson, 89–93. The Preacher's Toolbox. Peabody, MA: Hendrickson, 2012.

———. "The Place of Pathos in Preaching." *The Journal of the Evangelical Homiletics Society* 1, no. 1 (2001) 15–21.

———. *Preaching as Reminding: Stirring Memory in an Age of Forgetfulness.* Downers Grove, IL: IVP Academic, 2017.

Ashcroft, Bill, et al. *The Empire Writes Back: Theory and Practice in Post-Colonial Literatures.* London: Routledge, 1989. https://ereader.perlego.com/1/book/1614119/7.

Aune, Kristin. "Why Feminists Are Less Religious." *The Guardian,* March 30, 2011. http://www.theguardian.com/commentisfree/belief/2011/mar/29/why-feminists-less-religious-survey.

Baird, Julia. "The Church Stripped Bare: High Rate of Domestic Abuse among Anglicans Exposed." *Sydney Morning Herald,* June 12, 2021. https://www.smh.com.au/national/the-church-stripped-bare-high-rate-of-domestic-abuse-among-anglicans-exposed-20210611-p5809z.html.

———. "Domestic Violence in the Church: When Women are Believed Change Will Happen." *ABC News,* May 23, 2018. http://www.abc.net.au/news/2018-05-23/when-women-are-believed-the-church-will-change/9782184.

Baker, Kirk. "'The Power That Cannot Be Named': Jephthah's Daughter as a Vehicle of Story." *Canadian Theological Review* 1, no. 2 (2012) 68–80.

Bal, Mieke. "Dealing/with/Women: Daughters in the Book of Judges." In *Women in the Hebrew Bible: A Reader,* edited by Alice Bach, 317–34. New York: Routledge, 1999.

———. *Death and Dissymmetry: The Politics of Coherence in the Book of Judges.* Chicago: University of Chicago Press, 1988.

———. "Foreword." In *On Gendering Texts: Female and Male Voices in the Hebrew Bible,* edited by Athalya Brenner, et al., ix–xiii. Leiden: Brill, 1993.

———. "Introduction." In *Anti-Covenant: Counter-Reading Women's Lives in the Hebrew Bible,* edited by Mieke Bal, 11–24. Sheffield: Almond, 1989.

———. *Lethal Love: Feminist Literary Readings of Biblical Love Stories.* Bloomington: Indiana University Press, 1987.

———. *Murder and Difference: Gender, Genre, and Scholarship on Sisera's Death.* Indiana Studies in Biblical Literature. Bloomington: Indiana University Press, 1988.

Bal, Mieke, and Christine van Boheemen. *Narratology: Introduction to the Theory of Narrative.* Toronto: University of Toronto Press, 1985.

Bal, Mieke, and David Jobling. *On Story-Telling: Essays in Narratology.* Foundations and Facets Literary Facets. Sonoma: Polebridge, 1991.

Barr, Beth Allison. *The Making of Biblical Womanhood.* Grand Rapids: Brazos, 2021.

Bartholomew, Craig G. "Philosophy and Old Testament Interpretation: A Neglected Influence." In *Hearing the Old Testament: Listening for God's Address,* edited by Craig G. Bartholomew et al., 45–66. Grand Rapids: Eerdmans, 2012.

Bausch, William J. *Storytelling: Imagination and Faith.* Mystic, CT: Twenty-Third, 1984.

Bebbington, David. "The Nature of Evangelical Religion." In *Evangelicals: Who They Have Been, Are Now, and Could Be,* edited by David W. Bebbington et al., 31–55. Grand Rapids: Eerdmans, 2019.

Beldman, David J. H. *Judges.* The Two Horizons Old Testament Commentary. Grand Rapids: Eerdmans, 2020.

Benckhuysen, Amanda W. *The Gospel According to Eve.* Downers Grove, IL: InterVarsity, 2019.

Bessey, Sarah. *Jesus Feminist.* New York: Howard, 2013.

Bevan, Robert. *The Destruction of Memory: Architecture at War.* 2nd ed. London: Reaktion, 2016. https://ereader.perlego.com/1/book/777007/4.

Biddle, Mark E. *Reading Judges: A Literary and Theological Commentary*. Macon, GA: Smyth & Helwys, 2012.

Bilezikian, Gilbert G. *Beyond Sex Roles: What the Bible Says About a Woman's Place in Church and Family*. 3rd ed. Grand Rapids: Baker Academic, 2006.

Billings, J. Todd. *The Word of God for the People of God: An Entryway to the Theological Interpretation of Scripture*. Grand Rapids: Eerdmans, 2010.

Block, Daniel I. *Judges, Ruth*. Nashville: B & H, 1999.

Boda, Mark J. "Biblical Theology and Old Testament Interpretation." In *Hearing the Old Testament: Listening for God's Address*, edited by Craig G. Bartholomew et al., 122–53. Grand Rapids: Eerdmans, 2012.

Boda, Mark J., and George Schwab. *Judges, Ruth*. Grand Rapids: Zondervan, 2017.

Boer, Roland. *Last Stop before Antarctica: The Bible and Postcolonialism in Australia*. 2nd ed. Society of Biblical Literature Semeia Studies. Atlanta: Society of Biblical Literature, 2008.

Boling, Robert G. *Judges*. The Anchor Bible. Garden City, NY: Doubleday, 1975.

Bond, L. Susan. *Trouble with Jesus: Women, Christology and Preaching*. St. Louis: Chalice, 1999.

Boyd, Gregory A. *The Crucifixion of the Warrior God: Interpreting the Old Testament's Violent Portraits of God in Light of the Cross*. Volumes 1 and 2. Minneapolis: Fortress, 2017.

———. *The Myth of a Christian Nation: How the Quest for Political Power Is Destroying the Church*. Grand Rapids: Zondervan, 2005.

Brenner, Athalya. *A Feminist Companion to Judges*. Sheffield: JSOT, 1993.

———. *Judges: A Feminist Companion to the Bible*. Feminist Companion to the Bible. Sheffield: Sheffield Academic, 1999.

———. "A Triangle and a Rhombus in Narrative Structure: A Proposed Integrative Reading of Judges 4 and 5." *Vetus Testamentum* 40, no. 2 (1990) 129–38.

Brenner, Athalya, and Fokkelien van Dijk Hemmes. *On Gendering Texts: Female and Male Voices in the Hebrew Bible*. Leiden: Brill, 1993.

Brenner, Athalya, and Gale A. Yee, eds. *Joshua and Judges*. Texts@Contexts. Minneapolis: Fortress, 2013.

Brensinger, Terry L. *Judges*. Believers Church Bible Commentary. Scottdale, PA: Herald, 1999.

Brettler, Marc Zvi. *The Book of Judges*. London: Routledge, 2001.

Briggs, Richard. *The Virtuous Reader: Old Testament Narrative and Interpretive Virtue*. Grand Rapids: Baker Academic, 2010.

———. *Words in Action: Speech Act Theory and Biblical Interpretation. Toward a Hermeneutic of Self-Involvement*. Edinburgh: T. & T. Clark, 2001.

Broadus, John Albert. *On the Preparation and Delivery of Sermons*. New and rev. ed. Edited by Jesse Burton Weatherspoon. New York: Harper & Row, 1944.

Brown, Austin Channing. "Climbing the Mountain of Injustice." *Evolving Faith* podcast, July 1, 2020. https://podcasts.apple.com/ca/podcast/climbing-mountain-injustice-austin-channing-brown/id1519314093?i=1000480908908.

Brown, Jeannine K. *Scripture as Communication*. Grand Rapids: Baker Academic 2007.

Brown, Paul E. *The Holy Spirit: The Spirit's Interpreting Role in Relation to Biblical Hermeneutics*. Fearn: Mentor, 2002.

Brown, Sally A. "Designing the Sermon's Form." In *Ways of the Word: Learning to Preach for Your Time and Place*, edited by Sally A. Brown et al., 151–82. Minneapolis: Fortress, 2016.

———. "The Preacher as Interpreter of Word and World." In *Ways of the Word: Learning to Preach for Your Time and Place*, edited by Sally A. Brown et al., 99–122. Minneapolis: Fortress, 2016.

Brueggemann, Walter. *The Practice of Prophetic Imagination: Preaching an Emancipating Word*. Minneapolis: Fortress, 2012.

———. *Redescribing Reality: What We Do When We Read the Bible*. London: SCM, 2009.

Bucar, Liz. *Stealing My Religion: Not Just Any Cultural Appropriation*. Cambridge: Harvard University Press, 2022.

Buchanan, John M. "The 'I' in Sermons." *Christian Century*, June 3, 2007, 4. https://www.christiancentury.org/article/2007-03/i-sermons.

Budden, Chris. *Following Jesus in Invaded Space: Doing Theology on Aboriginal Land*. Princeton Theological Monograph Series. Eugene, OR: Pickwick, 2009.

Buechner, Frederick. *Telling the Truth: The Gospel as Tragedy, Comedy and Fairy Tale*. San Francisco: Harper & Row, 1977.

Burge, Gary M. *Whose Land? Whose Promise? What Christians Are Not Being Told About Israel and the Palestinians*. Rev. and updated ed. Cleveland: Pilgrim, 2013.

Bushur, James G. "The Early Christian Appropriation of Old Testament Scripture: The Canonical Reading of Scripture in 1 Clement." *Concordia Theological Quarterly* 83, no. 1–2 (2019) 63–83. http://www.ctsfw.net/media/pdfs/BushurEarlyChristian AppropriationofOldTestamentScripture.pdf.

Butler, Trent C. "Joshua-Judges and Postcolonial Criticism." In *Joshua and Judges*, edited by Athalya Brenner et al., 27–38. Minneapolis: Fortress, 2013.

———. *Judges*. Word Biblical Commentary. Grand Rapids: Zondervan, 2009.

Buttrick, David. *Homiletic: Moves and Structures*. London: SCM, 1987.

Calvin, Jean (John). *Calvin's Institutes*. MacDill, FL: MacDonald, 1509–64.

Campbell, Constantine R. *Jesus V. Evangelicals: A Biblical Critique of a Wayward Movement*. Grand Rapids: Zondervan, 2023.

Capill, Murray. *The Heart Is the Target: Preaching Practical Application from Every Text*. Phillipsburg, NJ: P&R, 2014.

Chan, Sam. *Preaching as the Word of God: Answering an Old Question with Speech-Act Theory*. Eugene, OR: Pickwick, 2016.

Chapell, Bryan. *Christ-Centered Preaching: Redeeming the Expository Sermon*. Grand Rapids: Baker Academic, 2005.

———. *Christ-Centered Sermons: Models of Redemptive Preaching*. 2nd ed. Grand Rapids: Baker Academic, 2005.

Chasin, Barbara H., and Laura Kramer. "Ageism and Sexism: Invisibility and Erasure." In *Gender Visibility and Erasure*, edited by Marcia Texler Segal et al. Bingley: Advances in Gender Research. Emerald, 2022. https://ereader.perlego.com/1/book/3270123/1?element_originalid=EMST6.

Cheney, Emily. *She Can Read: Feminist Reading Strategies for Biblical Narrative*. Valley Forge, PA: Trinity International, 1996.

Chenoweth, Ben. "The Pedagogy of Biblical Fiction: Where Research and Creativity Collide." In *Wondering About God Together*, edited by Les Ball et al., 284–302. Macquarie Park: SCD, 2018.

"Chicago Statement on Biblical Inerrancy." 1978. https://defendinginerrancy.com/chicago-statements/.

Chisholm, Robert B., Jr. *A Commentary on Judges and Ruth.* Grand Rapids: Kregel, 2013.

Chopp, Rebecca S. *The Power to Speak: Feminism, Language, God.* New York: Crossroad, 1989.

"Churches Where Women Preach in Australia." Fixinghereyes, 2016. http://www.fixinghereyes.org/women-preaching.

Claassens, L. Juliana M. *Mourner, Mother, Midwife: Reimagining God's Delivering Presence in the Old Testament.* Louisville: Westminster John Knox, 2012.

"Common Grace." https://www.commongrace.org.au/.

Compton, Julie. "Should Straight Actors Still Play Gay Characters? 'It's Complicated.'" January 2, 2021. https://www.nbcnews.com/feature/nbc-out/should-straight-actors-still-play-gay-characters-it-s-complicated-n1252603.

Conway, Mary C. *Judging the Judges: A Narrative Appraisal Analysis.* University Park, PA: Eisenbrauns, 2020.

Cooper, Jodie. "When the Wrath of Jodie Met the Grace of God." February 26, 2021. https://au.thegospelcoalition.org/article/when-the-wrath-of-jodie-met-the-grace-of-god/.

Craddock, Fred B. *As One Without Authority.* 3rd ed. Nashville: Abingdon, 1979.

———. *Preaching.* Nashville: Abingdon, 1985.

Crotts, Jeffrey. *Illuminated Preaching: The Holy Spirit's Vital Role in Unveiling His Word, the Bible.* Leominster: Day One, 2010.

Cundall, Arthur Ernest, and Leon Morris. *Judges.* Tyndale Old Testament Commentaries. London: Tyndale, 1968.

Curtice, Kaitlin B. *Native: Identity, Belonging, and Rediscovering God.* Grand Rapids: Brazos, 2020.

Davidson, Lisa Wilson. *Preaching the Women of the Bible.* Saint Louis: Chalice, 2006.

Davis, Dale Ralph. *Judges: Such a Great Salvation.* Expositor's Guide to the Historical Books. Grand Rapids: Baker, 1990.

DelCogliano, Radde-Gallwitz, et al., eds. *Works on the Spirit: Athanasius's Letters to Serapion on the Holy Spirit, and, Didymus's on the Holy Spirit.* Popular Patristics Series. Yonkers, NY: St. Vladimir's Seminary Press, 2011.

Derrida, Jacques. "Before the Law." In *Acts of Literature,* edited by Derek Attridge, 181–220. New York: Routledge, 1992.

Dickey, Brian. "Evangelical Anglicans Compared: Australia and Britain." In *Amazing Grace: Evangelicalism in Australia, Britain, Canada, and the United States,* edited by George A. Rawlyk et al., 215–40. Grand Rapids: Baker, 1993.

Dockery, David S., and Philip D. Wise. "Biblical Inerrancy: Pro or Con?" *The Theological Educator* 37 (Spring 1988) 15.

Donovan Turner, Mary, and Mary Lin Hudson. *Saved from Silence: Finding Women's Voice in Preaching.* St. Louis: Chalice, 1999.

Doriani, Daniel M. *Putting Truth to Work: The Theory and Practice of Biblical Application.* Phillipsburg, NJ: P & R, 2001.

Dube, Musa W. *Postcolonial Feminist Interpretation of the Bible.* St. Louis: Chalice, 2000.

Du Mez, Kristin Kobes. *Jesus and John Wayne: How White Evangelicals Corrupted a Faith and Fractured a Nation.* New York: Liveright, 2020.

Dunn, James D. G. "The Bible and Scholarship: On Bridging the Gap between the Academy and the Church." *Anvil* 19, no. 2 (2002) 109–18.

Durber, Susan. *Preaching Like a Woman*. London: SPCK, 2007.

Ebeling, Gerhard. *Theology and Proclamation: A Discussion with Rudolf Bultmann*. London: Collins, 1966.

Edwards, Aaron. *A Theology of Preaching and Dialectic: Scriptural Tension, Hearldic Proclamation and the Phenumatotological Moment*. London: Bloomsbury T. & T. Clark, 2018.

Edwards, J. Kent. *Effective First-Person Biblical Preaching: The Steps from Text to Narrative Sermon*. Grand Rapids: Zondervan, 2005.

Egan, Frances, and Beth Kearney. "How Autofiction Turns the Personal into the Political." January 11, 2023. https://theconversation.com/how-autofiction-turns-the-personal-into-the-political-192180.

Embry, Brad. "Narrative Loss, the (Important) Role of Women, and Community in Judges 19." In *Joshua and Judges*, edited by Athalya Brenner et al., 257–73. Minneapolis: Fortress, 2013.

Enns, Peter. *Inspiration and Incarnation: Evangelicals and the Problem of the Old Testament*. Grand Rapids: Baker Academic, 2005.

Erickson, Diandra Chretain. "Judges." In *Postcolonial Commentary and the Old Testament*, edited by Hemchand Gossai, 122–41. London: Bloomsbury, 2018.

Esler, Philip Francis. *Sex, Wives, and Warriors: Reading Old Testament Narrative with Its Ancient Audience*. Cambridge: James Clarke & Co., 2012.

Evans, Mary J. *Judges and Ruth*. Tyndale Old Testament Commentaries. Downers Grove, IL: InterVarsity, 2017.

Evans, Rachel Held. *Inspired: Slaying Giants, Walking on Water, and Loving the Bible Again*. Nashville: Nelson, 2018.

Exum, J. Cheryl. "Feminist Criticism: Whose Interests Are Being Served?" In *Judges & Method: New Approaches in Biblical Studies*, edited by Gale A. Yee, 65–89. Minneapolis: Fortress, 2007.

———. "On Judges 11." In *A Feminist Companion to Judges*, edited by Athalya Brenner, 131–44. Sheffield: JSOT, 1993.

———. *Plotted, Shot, and Painted: Cultural Representations of Biblical Women*. Sheffield: Sheffield Academic, 1996.

Faley, Roland J. *Joshua, Judges*. New Collegeville Bible Commentary. Collegeville, MN: Liturgical, 2011.

Fewell, Danna Nolan. "Deconstructive Criticism: Ashsah and the (E)Razed City of Writing." In *Judges & Method: New Approaches in Biblical Studies*, edited by Gale A. Yee, 115–37. Minneapolis: Fortress, 2007.

Flood, Alison. "Publishers Defend American Dirt as Claims of Cultural Appropriation Grow." *The Guardian*, January 25, 2020. https://www.theguardian.com/books/2020/jan/24/publishers-defend-american-dirt-claims-cultural-appropriation-jeanine-cummins-oprah.

Florence, Anna Carter. *Preaching as Testimony*. Louisville: Westminster John Knox, 2007.

Foskett, Mary F. *Interpreting the Bible: Approaching the Text in Preparation for Preaching*. Elements of Preaching. Philadelphia: Fortress, 2009.

Foucault, Michel. "What Is an Author?" In *Language, Counter-Memory, Practice: Selected Essays and Interviews*, edited by Donald F. Bouchard, 113–38. London: Cornell University Press, 1980.

Fowl, Stephen E. *Engaging Scripture: A Model for Theological Interpretation*. Challenges in Contemporary Theology. Malden, MA: Blackwell, 1998.

Frolov, Serge. *Judges*. The Forms of the Old Testament Literature. Grand Rapids: Eerdmans, 2013.

Fuchs, Esther. *Feminist Theory and the Bible: Interrogating the Sources*. London: Lexington, 2016.

———. "Jewish Feminist Approaches to the Bible." In *Women and Judaism: New Insights and Scholarship*, edited by Frederick E. Greenspahn, 25–40. New York: New York University Press, 2009.

———. *Sexual Politics in the Biblical Narrative: Reading the Hebrew Bible as a Woman*. Journal for the Study of the Old Testament Supplement Series. Sheffield: Sheffield Academic, 2000.

Funder, Anna. *Wifedom: Mrs Orwell's Invisible Life*. Hamish Hamilton: Penguin Australia, 2023.

Gadamer, Hans-Georg. *Truth and Method*. New York: Crossroad, 2013.

———. *Wahrheit Und Methode*. Tübingen: Mohr, 1965.

Gafney, Wilda C. *Womanist Midrash: A Reintroduction to the Women of the Torah and the Throne*. Louisville: Westminster John Knox, 2017.

Garner, Stephen Chapin. *Getting into Character: The Art of First-Person Narrative Preaching*. Grand Rapids: Brazos, 2008.

Genette, Gérard, and Jane E. Lewin. *Narrative Discourse: An Essay in Method*. Ithaca, NY: Cornell University Press, 1980.

Gerhardt, Elizabeth L. *The Cross and Gendercide: A Theological Response to Global Violence against Women and Girls*. Downers Grove, IL: InterVarsity, 2014.

Gignilliat, Mark, and Jonathan T. Pennington. "Theological Commentary." In *A Manifesto for Theological Interpretation*, edited by Craig G. Bartholomew et al., 237–56. Grand Rapids: Baker Academic, 2016.

Giles, Kevin. *What the Bible Actually Teaches on Women*. Eugene, OR: Cascade, 2018.

Goldingay, John. *Key Questions About Biblical Interpretation: Old Testament Answers*. Grand Rapids: Baker Academic, 2011.

———. *Models for Interpretation of Scripture*. Grand Rapids: Eerdmans, 1995.

Goldsworthy, Graeme. *Gospel-Centred Hermeneutics: Biblical-Theological Foundations and Principles*. Nottingham: Apollos, 2006.

———. *Preaching the Whole Bible as Christian Scripture*. Grand Rapids: Eerdmans, 2000.

Gossai, Hemchand, ed. *Postcolonial Commentary and the Old Testament*. London: Bloomsbury, 2018.

Gouldbourne, Ruth. "Not Just an Embodied Voice: Towards an Understanding of Preaching as an Embodied Practice." *Baptistic Theologies* 5, no. 1 (Spring 2013) 53–67.

Grenville, Kate. *The Writing Book: A Workbook for Fiction Writers*. Crows Nest: Allen & Unwin, 1990.

Greves, Abigail M. "Daughter of Courage: Reading Judges 11 with a Feminist Pentecostal Hermeneutic." *Journal of Pentecostal Theology* 25, no. 2 (2016) 151–67.

Grenz, Stanley J. *A Primer on Postmodernism*. Grand Rapids: Eerdmans, 1996.

Grenz, Stanley J., and Denise Muir Kjesbo. *Women in the Church: A Biblical Theology of Women in Ministry*. Downers Grove, IL: InterVarsity, 1995.

Griffith, Jessica Mesman. "A Dangerous Edge: Righteous Anger from Women Brings Hope, Not Despair." *U.S. Catholic* 83, no. 4 (2018) 38–39. https://search.ebscohost.com/login.aspx?direct=true&AuthType=ip,sso&db=rlh&AN=128185572&site=ehost-live&scope=site&custid=s9398328.

Gross, Nancy Lammers. *If You Cannot Preach Like Paul.* Grand Rapids: Eerdmans, 2002.

———. *Women's Voices and the Practice of Preaching.* Grand Rapids: Eerdmans, 2017.

Grudem, Wayne A. *Evangelical Feminism and Biblical Truth: An Analysis of 118 Disputed Questions.* Leicester: Apollos, 2004.

Grudem, Wayne A., and John Piper. *Recovering Biblical Manhood and Womanhood: A Response to Evangelical Feminism.* Wheaton, IL: Crossway, 1991.

Gunn, D. M. *Judges.* Oxford: Blackwell, 2005.

Gushee, David P. *After Evangelicalism: The Path to a New Christianity.* Louisville: Westminster John Knox, 2020.

Habermas, Jürgen. "A Review of Gadamer's Truth and Method." In *The Hermeneutic Tradition: From Ast to Ricoeur,* edited by Gayle L. Ormiston et al., 213–44. Albany: State University of New York Press, 1990.

Hall, Douglas John. "Who Tells the World's Story: Theology's Quest for a Partner in Dialogue." *Interpretation* 36, no. 1 (1982) 47–53.

Halsey. "A Story Like Mine." 2018. https://www.youtube.com/watch?v=Dpq8pHLhdVo.

Hamley, Isabelle M. *God of Justice and Mercy: A Theological Commentary on Judges.* London: SCM, 2021.

Hamlin, E. John. *At Risk in the Promised Land: A Commentary on the Book of Judges.* Grand Rapids: Eerdmans, 1990.

Harris, John. *One Blood: 200 Years of Aboriginal Encounter with Christianity: A Story of Hope.* Sutherland: Albatross, 1990.

Heaney, Robert S. "Prospects and Problems for Evangelical Postcolonialisms." In *Evangelical Postcolonial Conversations: Global Awakenings in Theology and Praxis,* edited by Kay Higuera Smith, 29–42. Downers Grove, IL: IVP Academic, 2014. https://ereader.perlego.com/1/book/3009226/4.

Heisler, Greg. *Spirit-Led Preaching: The Holy Spirit's Role in Sermon Preparation and Delivery.* Nashville: B&H Academic, 2007.

Helm, Paul. "The Idea of Inerrancy." In *The Enduring Authority of the Christian Scriptures,* edited by D. A. Carson, 899–919. London: Apollos, 2016.

Hiestand, Gerald, and Todd A. Wilson. *The Pastor Theologian: Resurrecting an Ancient Vision.* Grand Rapids: Zondervan, 2015.

Hjorth, Vigdis. *Is Mother Dead?* Translated by Charlotte Barslund. London: Verso, 2022.

———. *Will and Testament.* Translated by Charlotte Barslund. London: Verso, 2019.

Hirsch, E. D. *Validity in Interpretation.* London: Yale University Press, 1967.

Hodges, Louis Igou. "New Dimensions in Scripture." In *New Dimensions in Evangelical Thought: Essays in Honor of Millard J. Erickson,* edited by David Dockery, 209–34. Downers Grove, IL: InterVarsity, 1998.

Hogan, Lucy Lind, and Robert Reid. *Connecting with the Congregation: Rhetoric and the Art of Preaching.* Nashville: Abingdon, 1999.

Hoggard Creegan, Nicola, and Christine D. Pohl. *Living on the Boundaries: Evangelical Women, Feminism and the Theological Academy.* Downers Grove, IL: InterVarsity, 2005.

Holt, Robby, and Aubrey Spears. "The Ecclesia as Primary Context for the Reception of the Bible." In *A Manifesto for Theological Interpretation,* edited by Craig G. Bartholomew et al., 65–81. Grand Rapids: Baker Academic, 2016.

Hosanagar, Kartik. "Blame the Echo Chamber on Facebook. But Blame Yourself, Too." *Wired,* November 25, 2016. https://www.wired.com/2016/11/facebook-echo-chamber/.

Howard, Cameron B. R. *The Old Testament for a Complex World: How the Bible's Dynamic Testimony Points to New Life for the Church.* Grand Rapids: Baker Academic, 2021.

Japinga, Lynn. *Preaching the Women of the Old Testament.* Louisville: Westminster John Knox, 2017.

Jeter, Joseph R. Jr. *Preaching Judges.* St. Louis: Chalice, 2003.

Jeter, Joseph R. Jr., and Ronald J. Allen. *One Gospel, Many Ears: Preaching for Different Listeners in the Congregation.* St. Louis: Chalice, 2002.

Johnson, Darrell W. *The Glory of Preaching: Participating in God's Transformation of the World.* Downers Grove, IL: IVP Academic, 2009.

Johnson, Kimberly P. *The Womanist Preacher: Proclaiming Womanist Rhetoric from the Pulpit.* London: Lexington, 2017.

Johnston, Graham M. *Preaching to a Postmodern World: A Guide to Reaching Twenty-First Century Listeners.* Grand Rapids: Baker, 2001.

Jones-Warsaw, Koala. "Toward a Womanist Hermeneutic: A Reading of Judges 19–21." In *A Feminist Companion to Judges,* edited by Athalya Brenner, 172–86. Sheffield: Sheffield Academic, 1993.

Kahneman, Daniel. *Thinking, Fast and Slow.* New York: Farrar, Straus and Giroux, 2013.

Kaiser, Walter C., Jr. *Preaching and Teaching from the Old Testament: A Guide for the Church.* Grand Rapids: Baker Academic, 2003.

Kalmanofsky, Amy. *Gender-Play in the Hebrew Bible: The Ways the Bible Challenges Its Gender Norms.* New York: Routledge, 2017.

———. *The Power of Equivocation: Complex Readers and Readings of the Hebrew Bible.* Minneapolis: Fortress, 2022. https://ereader.perlego.com/1/book/3258060/8?element_originalid=ch01.

Kassian, Mary A. *The Feminist Mistake: The Radical Impact of Feminism on Church and Culture.* Wheaton, IL: Crossway, 2005.

Kay, James F. *Preaching and Theology.* St. Louis: Chalice, 2007.

Keefe, Alice A. "Tending the Fire of Anger: A Feminist Defense of a Much Maligned Emotion." *Buddhist-Christian Studies* 39 (2019) 67–76. https://doi.org/10.1353/bcs.2019.0006.

Keizer, Garret. *The Enigma of Anger: Essays on a Sometimes Deadly Sin.* San Francisco: Jossey-Bass, 2002.

Kim, Uriah Y. "The Politics of Othering in North America and in the Book of Judges." In *Postcolonial Theology,* edited by Hille Haker et al., 35–41. London: SCM, 2013.

———. "Postcolonial Criticism: Who Is the Other in the Book of Judges?" In *Judges and Methods: New Approaches in Biblical Studies,* edited by Gale A. Yee, 161–82. Minneapolis: Augsburg Fortress, 2007.

Klein, Lillian R. "Achsah: What Price This Prize?" In *Judges: A Feminist Companion to the Bible,* edited by Athalya Brenner, 18–26. Sheffield: Sheffield Academic, 1999.

———. "Paradigm and Deviation in Images of Women." In *A Feminist Companion to Judges,* edited by Athalya Brenner, 55–71. Sheffield: JSOT, 1993.

———. *The Triumph of Irony in the Book of Judges.* Bible and Literature Series. Sheffield: Almond, 1988.

Kostenberger, Margaret Elizabeth. *Jesus and the Feminists: Who Do They Say He Is?* Wheaton, IL: Crossway, 2008.

Kozaki, Danuta, and Alison Xiao. "Sydney Private School Students' Allegations of Sexual Assault in Online Petition 'Extremely Concerning.'" February 20, 2021. https://www.abc.net.au/news/2021-02-20/sydney-private-school-students-share-sexual-assault-experiences/13175058.

Kristof, Nicholas. "A Confession of Liberal Intolerance." *Sunday Review, New York Times,* May 7, 2016. https://www.nytimes.com/2016/05/08/opinion/sunday/a-confession-of-liberal-intolerance.html.

Kruger, Michael J. *Bully Pulpit: Confronting the Problem of Spiritual Abuse in the Church.* Grand Rapids: Zondervan, 2022.

Kuhatschek, Jack. *Taking the Guesswork out of Applying the Bible.* Downers Grove, IL: InterVarsity, 1990.

Kuruvilla, Abraham. *A Manual for Preaching: The Journey from Text to Sermon.* Grand Rapids: Baker Academic, 2019.

Kwok, Pui-lan. *Discovering the Bible in the Non-Biblical World.* Maryknoll, NY: Orbis, 1995.

———. *Postcolonial Imagination and Feminist Theology.* London: SCM, 2004.

Lake, Meredith. *The Bible in Australia: A Cultural History.* Sydney: NewSouth, 2018.

Lalitha, Jayachitra. "Postcolonial Feminism, the Bible and the Native Indian Woman." In *Evangelical Postcolonial Conversations: Global Awakenings in Theology and Praxis,* edited by Kay Higuera Smith, 75–87. Downers Grove, IL: IVP Academic, 2014.

Lane, Adrian. "Application and Persuasion: Bringing All of God's Word to All in His World." *Churchman* 127, no. 1 (Spring 2013) 55–70. http://churchsociety.org/churchman/archive.

Larsen, David L. *The Anatomy of Preaching: Identifying the Issues of Preaching Today.* Grand Rapids: Kregel, 1989.

Lauve-Moon, Katie. "Preacher Woman." In *Preacher Woman: A Critical Look at Sexism without Sexists,* edited by Katie Lauve-Moon, 165–86. New York: Oxford University Press, 2021.

Lee-Barnewall, Michelle. *Neither Complementarian nor Egalitarian: A Kingdom Correction to the Evangelical Gender Debate.* Grand Rapids: Baker Academic, 2016.

Lee, Ahmi. *Preaching God's Grand Drama: A Biblical-Theological Approach.* Grand Rapids: Baker Academic 2019.

Levine, Amy-Jill. "When the Bible Becomes Weaponized: Detecting and Disarming Jew-Hatred." *Studia Theologica* 75, no 2 (2021) 182–204. https://doi.org/10.1080/00393 38X.2021.1943256.

Levine, Amy-Jill, and Marc Zvi Bretter. *The Bible with and without Jesus: How Jews and Christians Read the Same Stories Differently.* New York: HarperCollins, 2020.

Lindsell, Harold. *The Battle for the Bible.* Grand Rapids: Zondervan, 1976.

Long, Thomas G. *Preaching and the Literary Forms of the Bible.* Philadelphia: Fortress, 1989.

———. "Taking the Listeners Seriously as the People of God." In *The Folly of Preaching: Models and Methods,* edited by Michael Knowles, 43–55. Grand Rapids: Eerdmans, 2007.

———. *The Witness of Preaching.* 2nd ed. Louisville: Westminster John Knox, 2005.

Lose, David J. *Confessing Jesus Christ: Preaching in a Postmodern World.* Grand Rapids: Eerdmans, 2003.

———. *Preaching at the Crossroads: How the World and Our Preaching Is Changing.* Minneapolis: Fortress, 2013.

Lovell, George, and Neil Richardson. *Sustaining Preachers and Preaching: A Practical Guide.* London: T. & T. Clark, 2011.

Lozano, Gilberto, and Federico A. Roth. "The Problem and Promise of Praxis in Postcolonial Criticism." In *Evangelical Postcolonial Conversations: Global Awakenings in Theology and Praxis*, edited by Kay Higuera Smith, 183–96. Downers Grove, IL: IVP Academic, 2014.

Lugashenko, Melissa. *Too Much Lip*. St Lucia: University of Queensland Press, 2018.

Lyotard, Jean-Francois. *The Postmodern Condition: A Report on Knowledge*. Theory and History of Literature 10. Translated by Geoff Bennington and Brian Massumi. Minneapolis: University of Minnesota Press, 1984.

MacArthur, John. "The Mandate of Biblical Inerrancy: Expository Preaching." *The Master's Seminary Journal* 1, no. 1 (Spring 1990) 3–15.

MacBride, Tim. *Catching the Wave: Preaching the New Testament as Rhetoric*. London: Inter-Varsity, 2016.

MacIntyre, Alasdair C. *Whose Justice? Which Rationality?* London: Duckworth, 1988.

Maiden, Samantha. "Young Staffer Brittany Higgins Says She Was Raped at Parliament House." news.com.au, February 15, 2021. https://www.news.com.au/national/politics/parliament-house-rocked-by-brittany-higgins-alleged-rape/news-story/fb02a5e95767ac306c51894fe2d63635.

Markham, Ian S., and Crystal J. Hardin, eds. *Prophetic Preaching: The Hope or the Curse of the Church?* New York: Church, 2020.

Martin, James Davidson. *The Book of Judges*. Cambridge Bible Commentary: New English Bible. Cambridge: Cambridge University Press, 1975.

Matthew, R. Malcolm. "'All That the Prophets Have Declared.'" In *All That the Prophets Have Declared: The Appropriation of Scripture in the Emergence of Christianity*, edited by R. Malcolm Matthew, xi–xii. Milton Keynes: Paternoster, 2015.

Matthews, Victor Harold. *Judges and Ruth*. Cambridge: Cambridge University Press, 2004.

Mathewson, Steven D. *The Art of Preaching Old Testament Narrative*. Grand Rapids: Baker Academic, 2002.

Matur, Bejan. "Every Woman Knows Her Own Tree." Translated by Canan Marasligil. Poetry Translation Centre. https://www.poetrytranslation.org/poems/every-woman-knows-her-own-tree.

McCann, J. Clinton. *Judges*. Louisville: Westminster John Knox, 2002.

McCaulley, Esau. *Reading While Black*. Downers Grove, IL: InterVarsity, 2020.

McClintock, Anne. *Imperial Leather: Race, Gender and Sexuality in the Colonial Contest*. London: Routledge, 1995.

McClure, John S. *Other-Wise Preaching: A Postmodern Ethic for Homiletics*. St. Louis: Chalice, 2001.

———. *The Roundtable Pulpit: Where Leadership and Preaching Meet*. Nashville: Abingdon, 1995.

McCullough, Amy Peed. *Her Preaching Body: Conversations About Identity, Agency, and Embodiment among Contemporary Female Preachers*. Eugene, OR: Cascade, 2018.

McGrath, Alister E. "Theology and the Futures of Evangelicalism." In *The Futures of Evangelicalism: Issues and Prospects*, edited by Craig G. Bartholomew et al., 15–39. Leicster: Inter-Varsity, 2003.

McKenzie, Alyce M. "At the Intersection of *Actio Divina* and *Homo Performans*." In *Performance in Preaching: Bringing the Sermon to Life*, edited by Jana Childers et al., 53–66. Grand Rapids: Baker Academic, 2008.

McKinlay, Judith E. "Meeting Achsah on Achsah's Land." *The Bible & Critical Theory* 5, no. 3 (2009) 39.1–.11. https://bibleandcriticaltheory.com/issues/vol5-no3/vol-5-no-3-2009-meeting-achsah-on-achsahs-land/.

McKnight, Edgar V. *Postmodern Use of the Bible: The Emergence of Reader-Oriented Criticism.* Nashville: Abingdon, 1988.

Merrick, Garret, et al., eds. *Five Views on Biblical Inerrancy, Counterpoints: Bible and Theology.* Grand Rapids: Zondervan, 2013.

Millar, Gary, and Phill Campbell. *Saving Eutychus: How to Preach God's Word and Keep People Awake.* Kingsford, AU: Matthias Media, 2013.

Mills, Paul. *Writing in Action.* New York: Routledge, 2002.

Milne, Pamela J. "From the Margins to the Margins: Jephthah's Daughter and Her Father." In *Joshua and Judges,* edited by Athalya Brenner et al., 209–34. Minneapolis: Fortress, 2013.

Mitchell, Basil. *How to Play Theological Ping-Pong: And Other Essays on Faith and Reason.* London: Hodder and Stoughton, 1990.

Mitchell, Henry H. "Emotion and Preaching: A Clarification." *The Living Pulpit* 15, no. 3 (2006) 26–8. https://web.p.ebscohost.com/ehost/pdfviewer/pdfviewer?vid=6&sid=aaf51ee4-249b-4fae-83be-81c309c7dcc4%40redis.

Moberly, R. W. L. "Preaching Christ from the Old Testament." In *Reclaiming the Old Testament for Christian Preaching,* edited by Grenville J. R. Kent et al., 233–50. Downers Grove, IL: InterVarsity, 2010.

Moore, Russell D. "After Patriarchy, What? Why Egalitarians Are Winning the Gender Debate." *Journal of the Evangelical Theological Society* 49, no. 3 (2006) 569–76.

Moore, Stephen D., and Fernando F. Segovia. *Postcolonial Biblical Criticism: Interdisciplinary Intersections.* London: T. & T. Clark, 2005.

Moreau, Jordan. "Halle Berry Pulls Out of Transgender Film Role After Backlash." *Variety,* July 6, 2020. https://variety.com/2020/film/news/halle-berry-trans-role-apology-transgender-film-1234699605/#!.

Mullner, Ilse. "Lethal Differences: Sexual Violence against Others in Judges 19." In *Judges: A Feminist Companion to the Bible,* edited by Athalya Brenner, 126–42. Sheffield: Sheffield Academic, 1999.

Murray, David P. *How Sermons Work.* Darlington: EP, 2011.

Naden, Neville. "Aboriginal Land and Australia's First Nations Peoples: Calling for Treaty, Recognition, and Engagement." In *Postcolonial Voices from Downunder: Indigenous Matters, Confronting Readings,* edited by Jione Havea, 46–57. Eugene, OR: Pickwick, 2017.

Naselli, Andrew David, and Collin Hansen, eds. *Four Views On: The Spectrum of Evangelicalism.* Grand Rapids: Zondervan, 2011.

Nausner, Michael. "Homeland as Borderland: Territories of Christian Subjectivity." In *Postcolonial Theologies: Divinity and Empire,* edited by Catherine Keller et al., 118–33. St. Louis: Chalice, 2004.

Neuger, Christie Cozad. "Image and Imagination: Why Inclusive Language Matters." In *Engaging the Bible in a Gendered World: An Introduction to Feminist Biblical Interpretation in Honor of Katharine Doob Sakenfeld,* edited by Linda Day et al., 153–65. London: Westminster John Knox, 2006.

Neusner, Jacob. *What Is Midrash?* Eugene, OR: Wipf and Stock, 2014.

Nietzsche, Friedrich. *The Will to Power.* Translated by Wilhelm, R. J. Hollingdale and Walter Arnold Kaufmann. Edited by Walter Kaufmann. New York: Vintage, 1968.

Noll, Mark A. *Between Faith and Criticism: Evangelicals, Scholarship and the Bible.* 2nd ed. Leicester: Apollos, 1991.

———. *The Rise of Evangelicalism: The Age of Edwards, Whitefield and the Wesleys.* Nottingham: Inter-Varsity, 2004.

———. *The Scandal of the Evangelical Mind.* Grand Rapids: Eerdmans, 1994.

Noth, Martin. *The History of Israel.* London: Adam & Charles Black, 1960.

O'Connell, Robert H. *The Rhetoric of the Book of Judges.* Supplements to Vetus Testamentum. New York: E. J. Brill, 1996.

O'Connor, Kathleen M. "The Feminist Movement Meets the Old Testament: One Woman's Perspective." In *Engaging the Bible in a Gendered World: An Introduction to Feminist Biblical Interpretation in Honor of Katharine Doob Sakenfeld,* edited by Katharine Doob Sakenfeld et al., 3–26. Louisville: Westminster John Knox, 2006.

Odell-Scott, David W. "Deconstruction." In *Handbook of Postmodern Biblical Interpretation,* edited by A. K. M. Adam, 55–61. St. Louis: Chalice, 2000.

Ortberg, John. "Biblical Preaching Is About Life Change, Not Sermon Form." In *The Art and Craft of Biblical Preaching: A Comprehensive Resource for Today's Communicators,* edited by Haddon W. Robinson et al., 451–53. Grand Rapids: Zondervan, 2005.

Osborne, Grant R. *The Hermeneutical Spiral.* 2nd ed. Downers Grove, IL: InterVarsity, 2006.

Packer, J. I. *"Fundamentalism" and the Word of God: Some Evangelical Principles.* Christian Classics Series. Leicester: Inter-Varsity, 1958.

Pasquarello, Michael, III. *Christian Preaching: A Trinitarian Theology of Proclamation.* Grand Rapids: Baker Academic, 2006.

Park, Song-Mi Suzie. "The World of the Judges in the Modern Context." *Word & World* 37, no. 3 (2017) 234–40.

Parry, Robin A. "Feminist Hermeneutics and Evangelical Concerns: The Rape of Dinah as a Case Study." In *Tamar's Tears: Evangelical Engagements with Feminist Old Testament Hermeneutics,* edited by Andrew Sloane, 30–64. Eugene, OR: Pickwick, 2012.

Pascoe, Bruce. *Dark Emu: Aboriginal Australia and the Birth of Agriculture.* Melbourne: Scribe, 2018.

Patterson, Sue M. *Realist Christian Theology in a Postmodern Age.* Cambridge: Cambridge University Press, 1999.

Paynter, Helen. *Telling Terror in Judges 19: Rape and Reparation for the Levite's Wife.* New York: Routledge, 2020. https://ereader.perlego.com/1/book/1480419/5.

Perdue, Carter, et al. *Israel and Empire: A Postcolonial History of Israel and Early Judaism.* Biblical Studies. London: Bloomsbury T. & T. Clark, 2015.

Peterson, Amy. *Where Goodness Still Grows: Reclaiming Virtue in an Age of Hypocrisy.* Nashville: Thomas Nelson, 2020.

Pierce, Ronald W., and Rebecca Merrill Groothuis, eds. *Discovering Biblical Equality: Complementarity without Hierarchy.* Leicester: Apollos, 2005.

Plantinga, Alvin. *Warrant and Proper Function.* New York: Oxford University Press, 1993.

Porter, Stanley E. "The Authority of the Bible as a Hermeneutical Issue." *Evangelical Quarterly* 86, no. 4 (2014) 303–24.

Powell, Mark Allan. *What Do They Hear? Bridging the Gap between Pulpit and Pew.* Nashville: Abingdon, 2007.

Powell, R., and M. Pepper. "National Anglican Family Violence Research Report: Top Line Results." Anglican Church of Australia (NCLS Research: April 2021). https://anglican.org.au/wp-content/uploads/2021/06/NAFVP-Top-Line-Results-Report-NCLS-Research.pdf.

Prentis, Brooke. "Walking Together." Seaforth Baptist Church, July 5, 2020.

Price, Jacinta Nampijinpa. "'Black Lives Matter' Is Not the Answer." June 18, 2021. https://www.jacintaprice.com/black_lives_matter_is_not_the_answer.

Prior, Michael. *The Bible and Colonialism: A Moral Critique*. Biblical Seminar. Sheffield: Sheffield Academic, 1997.

Quicke, Michael J. *360-Degree Preaching: Hearing, Speaking, and Living the Word*. Grand Rapids: Baker Academic, 2003.

Raiter, Michael. "On Sermons and Preaching." *St Mark's Review*, no. 219 (2012) 72–85. https://search.ebscohost.com/login.aspx?direct=true&AuthType=ip,sso&db=lsdar&AN=ATLA0001887832&site=ehost-live&scope=site&custid=s9398328.

Ratner, Tsila. "Playing Fathers' Games: The Story of Achsah, Daughter of Caleb, and the Princess's Blank Sheet." *Journal of Modern Jewish Studies* 3, no. 2 (2004) 147–61. https://doi.org/10.1080/1472588042000225820.

Redwood, Christine. "Achsah's Memories, Women of the Bible." New City Church, September 3, 2023.

———. "Enough Is Enough, UnFinished." Seaforth Baptist Church, March, 21, 2021.

———. "Hear Their Voices, Unfinished: the Book of Judges." Seaforth Baptist Church, January 31, 2021.

———. "Kaleidoscopic Preaching: Incorporating Multiple Voices into an Evangelical Sermon." *Feminist Theology* 32, no. 1 (August 2023).

———. "The God Who Sees." Seaforth Baptist Church, January 28, 2018.

———. "Preaching and Postcolonialism in Australia." *St Mark's Review*, no. 258 (2021) 72–83.

———. "Resisting Bad Theology, UnFinished." Seaforth Baptist Church, February 28, 2021.

———. "The Road to Emmaus, Gospel of Luke." Seaforth Baptist Church, April 12, 2020.

———. "The Silence of God, UnFinished." Seaforth Baptist Church, February 21, 2021.

———. "Storytelling, Images of Care." Seaforth Baptist Church, September 9, 2018.

Redwood, Christine, and Cherry Mawson. "Leah and Rachel, Amazing Grace." Seaforth Baptist Church, October 28, 2018.

Reed, Walter L. *Dialogues of the Word: The Bible as Literature According to Bakhtin*. New York: Oxford University Press, 1993.

Reid, Robert Stephen. *The Four Voices of Preaching*. Grand Rapids: Brazos, 2006.

Ricoeur, Paul. *Interpretation Theory: Discourse and the Surplus of Meaning*. Fort Worth: Texas Christian University Press, 1976.

———. "The World of the Text and the World of the Reader." Translated by Kathleen Blamey and David Pellauer. In *Time and Narrative*, vol. 3, edited by Paul Ricoeur, 157–79. Chicago: The University of Chicago Press, 1988.

The Rise and Fall of Mars Hill. Audio podcast, 2021–2022. https://www.christianitytoday.com/ct/podcasts/rise-and-fall-of-mars-hill/.

Robinson, Haddon. *Biblical Preaching: The Development and Delivery of Expository Messages*. 2nd ed. Grand Rapids: Baker, 2001.

———. "Listening to the Listeners." In *Changing Lives through Preaching and Worship*, edited by Marshall Shelley, 37–42. Nashville: Moorings, 1995.

Robinson, Haddon W., and Torrey W. Robinson. *It's All in How You Tell It: Preaching First-Person Expository Messages*. Grand Rapids: Baker, 2003.

Rose, Lucy Atkinson. *Sharing the Word: Preaching in the Roundtable Church*. Louisville: Westminster John Knox, 1997.

Ryan, Roger J. *Judges*. Sheffield: Sheffield Phoenix, 2007.

"Safer Spaces Toolkit: Addressing Domestic Abuse and Building Relationally Healthy Communities." Australian Baptist Ministries 2021. https://saferspacestoolkit.com.au/.

Sakenfeld, Katharine Doob. "Whose Text Is It?" *Journal of Biblical Literature* 127, no. 1 (Spring 2008) 3–18.

Sanders, Cheryl J. "The Woman as Preacher." In *A Reader on Preaching: Making Connections*, edited by David Day et al., 211–23. Aldershot: Ashgate, 2005.

Sasson, Jack M. *Judges 1–12*. The Anchor Yale Bible. New Haven: Yale University Press, 2014.

Saunders, Isabella. "Post-Colonial Australia: Fact or Fabrication?" *NEW: Emerging Scholars in Australian Indigenous Studies* 2, no. 1 (2018) 56–61.

Scheib, Karen D. *Challenging Invisibility: Practices of Care with Older Women*. St. Louis: Chalice, 2004.

Schirato, Tony, and Susan Yell. *Communication and Cultural Literacy*. 2nd ed. St. Leonards: Allen Unwin, 2000.

Schleiermacher, Friedrich, and Heinz Kimmerle. *Hermeneutics: The Handwritten Manuscripts*. Missoula, MT: Scholars, 1977.

Schneider, Tammi J. *Judges*. Collegeville, MN: Liturgical, 2000.

Schwartz, Regina M. *The Curse of Cain: The Violent Legacy of Monotheism*. Chicago: University of Chicago Press, 1997.

Scott, Jeremy. "Restorying: The Creative Act of Retelling." In *Narrative Retellings: Stylistic Approaches*, edited by Marina Lambrou, 23–44. London: Bloomsbury Academic, 2020.

Segovia, Fernando F. "Mapping the Postcolonial Optic in Biblical Criticism: Meaning and Scope." In *Postcolonial Biblical Criticism: Interdisciplinary Intersections*, edited by Stephen D. Moore et al., 23–78. London: T. & T. Clark, 2005.

Segovia, Fernando F., and Mary Ann Tolbert. *Reading from This Place*. Minneapolis: Fortress, 1995.

Seitz, Christopher R. *The Elder Testament*. Waco, TX: Baylor University Press, 2018.

Shercliff, Liz. *Preaching Women: Gender, Power and the Pulpit*. London: SCM, 2019. https://ereader.perlego.com/1/book/1437545/2.

Shriver, Lionel. "Lionel Shriver's Full Speech: 'I Hope the Concept of Cultural Appropriation Is a Passing Fad.'" *Guardian Australia*, September 13, 2016. https://www.theguardian.com/commentisfree/2016/sep/13/lionel-shrivers-full-speech-i-hope-the-concept-of-cultural-appropriation-is-a-passing-fad.

Sider, Ronald J. *The Scandal of Evangelical Politics: Why Are Christians Missing the Chance to Really Change the World?* Grand Rapids: Baker, 2008.

Sloane, Andrew. *On Being a Christian in the Academy: Nicholas Wolterstorff and the Practice of Christian Scholarship*. Paternoster Biblical and Theological Monographs. Carlisle: Paternoster, 2003.

———."Wolterstorff, Exegetical Theorising and Interpersonal Relationships in Genesis 1–3 (Vol 1)." Doctor of Theology. Australian College of Theology, 1994.

Smith, Carol. "Delilah: A Suitable Case for (Feminist) Treatment?" In *Judges: A Feminist Companion to the Bible*, edited by Athalya Brenner, 93–116. Sheffield: Sheffield Academic, 1999.

Smith, Claire. *God's Good Design: What the Bible Really Says About Men and Women*. Kingsford: Matthias Media, 2012.

Smith, James K. A. *The Fall of Interpretation: Philosophical Foundations for a Creational Hermeneutic.* 2nd ed. Grand Rapids: Baker, 2012.

Smith, Kay Higuera. "Embracing the Other: A Vision for Evangelical Identity." In *Evangelical Postcolonial Conversations: Global Awakenings in Theology and Praxis,* edited by Kay Higuera Smith, 197–210. Downers Grove: IVP Academic, 2014.

Soggin, J. Alberto. *Judges: A Commentary.* Old Testament Library. London: SCM, 1981.

Sparks, Kenton L. *God's Word in Human Words: An Evangelical Appropriation of Critical Biblical Scholarship.* Grand Rapids: Baker Academic, 2008.

Sproul, R. C. *Scripture Alone: The Evangelical Doctrine.* Phillipsburg, NJ: P&R, 2005.

Ska, Jean Louis. "Our Fathers Have Told Us": Introduction to the Analysis of Hebrew Narratives.* Roma: Editrice Pontificio Instituto Biblico, 1990.

Stackhouse, John. "Generic Evangelicalism." In *Four Views On: The Spectrum of Evangelicalism,* edited by Andrew David Naselli et al., 116–42. Grand Rapids: Zondervan, 2011.

———. *Need to Know: Vocation as the Heart of Christian Epistemology.* New York: Oxford University Press, 2014.

Stanton, Elizabeth Cady. *The Woman's Bible.* Washington: Coalition Task Force on Women and Religion, 1974.

Steimle, Niedenthal, et al. *Preaching the Story.* Philadelphia: Fortress, 1980.

Stein, Robert H. *A Basic Guide to Interpreting the Bible: Playing by the Rules.* Grand Rapids: Baker Academic, 2011.

Stephens, John, and Robyn McCallum. "Pre-Texts, Metanarratives, and the Western Metaethic." In *Retelling Stories, Framing Culture: Traditional Story and Metanarratives in Children's Literature,* edited by John Stephens et al., 3–24. New York: Garland, 2013.

Stott, John R. W. *Between Two Worlds.* Grand Rapids: Eerdmans, 1982.

Strachan, Owen. "Divine Order in a Chaotic Age: On Women Preaching." Thought Life: Patheos, May 7, 2019. https://www.patheos.com/blogs/thoughtlife/2019/05/divine-order-in-a-chaotic-age-on-women-preaching/.

Strawn, Brent A. *Honest to God Preaching: Talking Sin, Suffering and Violence.* Minneapolis: Fortress, 2021. https://ereader.perlego.com/1/book/2582983.

Sugirtharajah, R. S. *Postcolonial Reconfigurations: An Alternative Way of Reading the Bible and Doing Theology.* London: SCM, 2003.

———. *Voices from the Margin: Interpreting the Bible in the Third World.* London: SPCK, 1991.

Sutton, Peter, and Keryn Walshe. *Farmers or Hunter-Gatherers? The Dark Emu Debate.* Melbourne: Melbourne University Press, 2021.

Swears, Thomas R. *Preaching to Head and Heart.* Nashville: Abingdon, 2000.

Swinton, John. *Dementia: Living in the Memories of God.* Grand Rapids: Eerdmans, 2012. https://ereader.perlego.com/1/book/2015802/3.

Tame, Grace. "Culture of Silence Keeps Abuse Systems in Place." *The Sydney Morning Herald,* March 6, 2021. https://www.smh.com.au/national/culture-of-silence-keeps-abuse-systems-in-place-20210305-p577zp.html.

Taylor, Mark C. *Erring: A Postmodern a/Theology.* Chicago: University of Chicago Press, 1984.

Taylor, W. David O. *Open and Unafraid: The Psalms as a Guide to Life.* Nashville: Nelson, 2020.

Thelle, Rannfrid I. "Matrices of Motherhood in Judges 5." *Journal for the Study of the Old Testament* 43, no. 3 (2019) 436–52.

Thiselton, Anthony C. "Authority and Hermeneutics: Some Proposals for a More Creative Agenda." In *A Pathway into the Holy Scripture*, edited by P. E. Satterthwaite et al., 107–42. Tyndale Fellowship for Biblical and Theological Research. Grand Rapids: Eerdmans, 1994.

———. *The Two Horizons: New Testament Hermeneutics and Philosophical Description with Special Reference to Heidegger, Bultmann, Gadamer, and Wittgenstein.* Exeter, UK: Paternoster, 1980.

Thompson, William D. *Preaching Biblically: Exegesis and Interpretation.* Nashville: Abingdon, 1981.

Tisdale, Leonora Tubbs. *Preaching as Local Theology and Folk Art.* Minneapolis: Augsburg Fortress, 1997.

Topsfield, Jewel. "Half of All Australian Women Sexually Harassed: Survey." *The Sydney Morning Herald*, December 7, 2021. https://www.smh.com.au/national/half-of-all-australian-women-sexually-harassed-survey-20211207-p59fd6.html.

Torrance, Thomas F. *Theological Science: Based on the Hewett Lectures for 1959.* London: Oxford University Press, 1978.

Traister, Rebecca. *Good and Mad: The Revolutionary Power of Women's Anger.* New York: Simon & Schuster, 2018.

Travis, Sarah. *Decolonizing Preaching: The Pulpit as Postcolonial Space.* Lloyd John Ogilvie Institute of Preaching Series. Eugene, OR: Cascade, 2014.

Trible, Phyllis. "Five Loaves and Two Fishes: Feminist Hermeneutics and Biblical Theology." *Theological Studies* 50, no. 2 (1989) 279–95.

———. *Texts of Terror: Literary-Feminist Readings of Biblical Narratives.* Philadelphia: Fortress, 1984.

Tuohy, Anne. "The History of Feminist Theology." In *Raising Women Leaders: Perspectives on Liberating Women in Pentecostal and Charismatic Contexts*, edited by Shane Clifton et al., 221–35. Chester Hill: Australasian Pentecostal Studies, 2009.

Tyler, Johanna Harris. "Submission to Your Husband Is a Dangerous Doctrine." *The Drum*, March 9, 2015. http://www.abc.net.au/news/2015-03-09/harris-submission-to-your-husband-is-a-dangerous-doctrine/6290304.

Van Harn, Roger. *Preacher, Can You Hear Us Listening?* Grand Rapids: Eerdmans, 2005.

Vanhoozer, Kevin J. *Is There a Meaning in This Text? The Bible, the Reader, and the Morality of Literary Knowledge.* Leicester: Apollos, 1998.

Van Til, Cornelius. *The Defense of the Faith.* Phillipsburg, NJ: Presbyterian and Reformed, 1955.

Vaux, Roland de. *The Early History of Israel, Vol. 2: To the Period of the Judges.* London: Darton, Longman & Todd, 1978.

Vulliamy, Ed. "Voices above the Chaos: Female War Poets from the Middle East." *The Guardian*, September 4, 2016. https://www.theguardian.com/books/2016/sep/04/female-poets-of-syrian-war-turkey-middle-east.

Ward, Richard F. "Performance Turns in Homiletics." *Reformed Liturgy and Music* 30 (1996). https://www.religion-online.org/article/performance-turns-in-homiletics/.

Wardlaw, Don M. "Preaching from Anger." *The Living Pulpit* 2, no. 4 (1993) 36–37. https://search.ebscohost.com/login.aspx?direct=true&AuthType=ip,sso&db=lsdar&AN=ATLA0000919358&site=ehost-live&scope=site&custid=s9398328.

Warfield, Benjamin Breckinridge, and Samuel G. Craig. *The Inspiration and Authority of the Bible*. Philadelphia: Presbyterian and Reformed, 1948.

Warrior, Robert Allen. "Canaanites, Cowboys, and Indians: Deliverance, Conquest, and Liberation Theology Today." *Christianity and Crisis* 49, no. 12 (1989) 261–65.

Way, Kenneth C. *Judges and Ruth*. Teach the Text: Commentary Series. Grand Rapids: Baker, 2016.

Webb, Barry G. *The Book of Judges*. The New International Commentary on the Old Testament. Grand Rapids: Eerdmans, 2012.

———. *Judges and Ruth: God in Chaos*. Preaching the Word. Wheaton, IL: Crossway, 2015.

Webb, Joseph. *Old Texts, New Sermons: The Quiet Revolution in Biblical Preaching*. St Louis: Chalice, 2000.

Webb, Stephen H. *The Divine Voice: Christian Proclamation and the Theology of Sound*. Grand Rapids: Brazos, 2004.

Webb, William J. *Slaves, Women and Homosexuals: Exploring the Hermeneutics of Cultural Analysis*. Downers Grove, IL: InterVarsity, 2001.

Wellhausen, Julius. *Prolegomena to the History of Israel*. Edinburgh: Adam & Charles Black, 1885.

Westphal, Merold. *Whose Community? Which Interpretation? Philosophical Hermeneutics for the Church*. The Church and Postmodern Culture. Grand Rapids: Baker Academic, 2009.

Whitehead, Evelyn Eaton, and James D. Whitehead. *Transforming Our Painful Emotions: Spiritual Resources in Anger, Shame, Grief, Fear, and Loneliness*. Maryknoll, NY: Orbis, 2010.

Whitelam, Keith W. *The Invention of Ancient Israel: The Silencing of Palestinian History*. London: Routledge, 1996.

Wilcock, Michael. *The Message of Judges: Grace Abounding*. Leicester: Inter-Varsity, 1992.

Williams, Michael E. "Preaching as Storytelling." In *Journeys toward Narrative Preaching*, edited by Wayne Bradley Robinson, 106–24. New York: Pilgrim, 1990.

Wilson, Stephen M. "Samson the Man-Child: Failing to Come of Age in the Deuteronomistic History." *Journal of Biblical Literature* 133, no. 1 (Spring 2014) 43–60.

Whitehead, Evelyn Eaton, and James D. Whitehead. *Transforming Our Painful Emotions: Spiritual Resources in Anger, Shame, Grief, Fear, and Loneliness*. Maryknoll, NY: Orbis, 2010.

Winch, Tara. *The Yield*. Hamish Hamilton: Penguin Random House Australia, 2019.

Witvliet, John D. *The Biblical Psalms in Christian Worship: A Brief Introduction and Guide to Resources*. Grand Rapids: Eerdmans, 2007.

Wolterstorff, Nicholas. *Divine Discourse*. Cambridge: Cambridge University Press, 1995.

Woodley, Randy S., and Bo C. Sanders. "Was Jesus an Evangelical, or Even Perhaps a Postcolonial Theologian?" In *Decolonizing Evangelicalism: An 11.59pm Conversation*, edited by Randy S. Woodley et al., 17–39. Eugene, OR: Cascade, 2020.

Woollacott, Angela, and Michelle Staff. "Sex, Power and Anger: A History of Feminist Protests in Australia." *The Conversation*, March 27, 2021. https://www.abc.net.au/news/2021-03-27/sex-power-and-anger-a-history-of-feminist-protests-in-australia/100030592.

Wright, Christopher J. H. *The Mission of God's People: A Biblical Theology of the Church's Mission*. Grand Rapids: Zondervan, 2010.

Wright, Jacob L. "Military Valor and Kingship: A Book-Oriented Approach to the Study of a Major War Theme." In *Writing and Reading War: Rhetoric, Gender, and Ethics in Biblical and Modern Contexts*, edited by Brad E. Kelle et al., 33–56. Atlanta: Society of Biblical Literature, 2008.

———. *War, Memory, and National Identity in the Hebrew Bible*. Cambridge: Cambridge University Press, 2020.

Wright, John W. *Telling God's Story: Narrative Preaching for Christian Formation*. Downers Grove, IL: InterVarsity, 2007.

Wright, Nicholas Thomas. *The New Testament and the People of God*. London: SPCK, 1992.

Wurtzel, Elizabeth. *Bitch: In Praise of Difficult Women*. New York, 1998.

Younger, K. Larsen Jr. *Judges and Ruth*. NIV Application Commentary: From Biblical Text to Contemporary Life. Grand Rapids: Zondervan, 2002.

Yuval-Davis, Anthias, et al. *Woman–Nation–State*. Basingstoke: Macmillan, 1989.

Zimmermann, Jens. *Recovering Theological Hermeneutics: An Incarnational-Trinitarian Theory of Interpretation*. Grand Rapids: Baker Academic, 2004.

9781666780956